Praise for Mov
through Grief

For anyone whose heart is heavy from grief of any kind, you must read this book, *Moving from Broken to Beautiful® through Grief.* Not only has Yvonne Ortega walked where you are walking, she will take your hand and lead you to a place of healing, through the love and the power of Christ. I know because she has helped me.

Babbie Mason
Award-winning Singer, Songwriter, Author, and TV Talk Show Host

Knowing Yvonne these past forty years, I have witnessed, amidst her suffering and pain, a steadfast, obedient and faithful servant of God. Out of her deep sorrow and loss has come a life of fulfillment and purpose. Yvonne Ortega's life story, *Moving from Broken to Beautiful® through Grief*, is one I will treasure and recommend to the women I serve. I could not put it down. It came at a time when I needed it most!

Darlene Barber
Bible Study Fellowship Teaching Leader
Director of Women's Ministries—Shadow Mountain Community Church, El Cajon, California

When you are grieving, you do not want to go anywhere, talk to anyone, do anything, or read a book. However, Yvonne Ortega approaches grief with such a sensitive and heartfelt perspective that you want her to reach out and hold your hand. Sharing her personal experience in *Moving from Broken to Beautiful® through Grief,* Yvonne gently assures the reader that though the journey is long and painful, he or she can arrive at a new normal that includes joy and fulfillment and abundant living.

Linda Gilden
Author, Speaker, Writing Coach

As one who is all too familiar with grief, author Yvonne Ortega has penned yet another touching yet practical book about accepting grief and finding beauty in the midst of it. I, too, have experienced grief and have found the words of this book to be not only true, but healing. If you are struggling with the pain of loss, this book will guide you to a bittersweet place of victory.

Kathi Macias
Award-winning author of more than fifty books
Latest release, *A Husband's Christmas Prayer*

With wisdom and insight that can only come through unwanted experience, therapist Yvonne Ortega offers more than a sterile formula for dealing with the death of a loved one. Her heartfelt words and practical tools in *Moving from Broken to Beautiful® through Grief* provide a soothing balm for those suffering loss. It's as if Ortega is your best friend—beside you on the couch, arm around your shoulders, tissues in her hands. She knows. She understands. She's been where you are.

Vonda Skelton, Author and Speaker
Founder of Christian Communicators Conference

I immersed myself in Yvonne Ortega's book, *Moving from Broken to Beautiful® through Grief*, eight weeks after my beloved husband suddenly passed away. Yvonne's words ring true and gave me hope because she has walked and survived the raw brokenness of grief and pain. Through a well-balanced weaving of her own life's stories, along with substantiated selection of Scriptures, Yvonne created the perfect mix for guiding the readers into their beautiful future. This book is the essential healing oil for any person walking a journey of grief or brokenness.

Heidi McLaughlin, International Speaker and Author *Restless for More, Beauty Unleashed,* and *Sand to Pearls*

Yvonne Ortega has done it again with her beautifully written, *Moving from Broken to Beautiful® through Grief.* This is Yvonne's fourth book in her *Moving from Broken to Beautiful® series*, and is perhaps her most powerful.

You feel Yvonne's arms wrap around you as she shares the details of her painful journey, providing wisdom and encouragement to her readers. What I love best are the practical and actionable ideas she provides for someone moving through grief.

At the end of each chapter, Yvonne offers Activities, Affirmations, Reading and Prayer, Music, and Journal suggestions to help the reader take action and move forward.

This book will be the perfect gift for any friend who is moving through grief. Highly recommended.

Cathy Fyock, The Business Book Strategist and Author *Blog2Book*

Raw. Real. Relentless. Recovery. Such is author Yvonne Ortega's dialogue with us on her healing grief journey in her latest release: *Moving from Broken to Beautiful® through Grief.* This skillfully crafted resource offers handles for emotions and titles for those who attempt to join the grieving to process their pain. I was widowed at a tender age and learned much from people's often futile efforts to enter my loss. Ortega's term, "Wound Salters," helped me to process the comments of those who don't know what to say and think they should speak. Also helpful was the term "Comforting Angels," as she describes those who listened to God's instructions for how to help Ortega navigate through the swamp of the loss of her only child. With bravery, Ortega says, "Regardless of the cause of his death, I still lost my only child, and I'll never be a grandparent. My life took a different path than what I expected when Brian was first born. If you have lost a loved one, your path has changed too. How do you cope? How do you live the 'new normal' when you don't want it? You want your loved one back. How do you fight against and survive the new normal?" This heartfelt wisdom, thought-provoking journal entries and sound biblical wisdom are freely offered through this practical, genuine book. Buy one for yourself and several more to keep in your office to give away and offer hope and healing to those who are grieving.

Sheryl Giesbrecht, Author, Speaker, International Radio and TV Personality, Global Influencer

Moving from Broken to Beautiful® through Grief is a must-have resource, for yourself and to gift others in their times of need. Yvonne writes with such compassion, and from personal and professional experiences, she knows what she's talking about, and has done what she's suggesting. I related to this at the heart level, having lost cousins, an uncle and aunt, my business advisor, brother, father and mother, all within a short span of time. Anyone reading this book will feel genuinely comforted.

Sheryl Roush, Speaker, Author, *Heart of a Mother*

Yvonne Ortega's book, *Moving from Broken to Beautiful® through Grief,* gives the readers the needed perspective, examples, and helps to show them how to move through their journey of grief to healing.

Linda Evans Shepherd
Founder and President of the Advanced Writers and Speakers Association (AWSA)

Latest Release: *Winning Your Daily Spiritual Battles: Living Empowered by the Armor of God*

I have lost a loved one, not once, but on multiple occasions. I have journeyed through painful places, angry places, and places that I can only imagine hell feels like. The hole that is left behind is one that refuses to be filled, no matter how many people, relationships, or other self-medications you try to shove into it. Yvonne, somehow, has managed to transform her devastating loss into a testimony that walks the reader through each of those places and into true healing. Her approach is gentle, yet raw and powerful. This is more than just a book you read. It is an experience. It is more like a testimony that serves as a map through the process of healing. It will help you uncover and work through areas you had not been able to before, and in some cases, didn't even know existed. You will feel comforted that someone else had some of the same feelings you feel ashamed of sometimes, but you see now are just a part of the process. Thank you, Yvonne, for sharing such a vulnerable experience with this world, so that we can learn to move from broken to beautiful through grief, as you have.

Courtney C. Buzzell
Proximo Marketing Strategies, Owner
Peninsula Women's Network, President

If you feel like there is no way back from sorrow and pain, read *Moving from Broken to Beautiful®*

through Grief with an open heart, and you'll discover that God's power is made perfect in your weakness. Ortega's ability to weave the timeless Scriptures in with her powerful and relatable testimony is a combination that will prove vital for those who want to experience the joy of Christ in suffering.

Rev. Michael Howard
Seaford Baptist Church—Seaford, Virginia

Sometimes our world gets shattered, and we don't even know where to begin picking up the pieces. Sometimes, we may not even want to go through the grieving process. However, what if I told you that you could find peace on the other side of this pain? What if you could find purpose from the pain? What if you could even find promise? Would you go on that journey? If so, this is the book for you. In *Moving from Broken to Beautiful® through Grief*, Yvonne Ortega shows you how to not only pick up the pieces, but to build a whole new beautiful life. Believe me, it will be worth it.

Craig Valentine
1999 Toastmasters World Champion of Public Speaking, Author, *World Class Speaking*

The gift of the "wounded healer" is offered by Yvonne Ortega as she companions her readers in *Moving from Broken to Beautiful® through Grief*. Ms. Ortega not only poignantly reveals her own experience in this journey from devastation and loss to finally a move toward integration and healing, but she also skillfully employs both her clinical awareness of the grieving process and her Christian beliefs to add a foundation to the process. It is said that "none of us get out of this alive," and thus we all experience loss and grief. Grief as a part of life is a relational experience. Ms. Ortega's latest book provides a comforting support for those who are currently in the disturbance of acute grief and an excellent guide to those who are at this point in the position of comforter and friend.

Carolyn Griffith
Licensed Professional Counselor and Spiritual Director Touchstones Counseling

Moving from Broken to Beautiful® through Grief is the fourth book in Yvonne Ortega's series, *Moving from Broken to Beautiful®*. It is another masterful expression of personal insight and experience. This work is a generously transparent journey of how the author moved from the brokenness of her own loss to the beautiful wholeness and resurrection life found in the Holy Scriptures.

Laura Seibert, ACG, ALB
District 66 Division D Director 2015-2016, Toastmasters International

In her latest book, *Moving from Broken to Beautiful® through Grief*, Yvonne Ortega walks her readers through the valley of the shadow of death. She knows from hard-won experience that it doesn't work to try and bottle up grief nor to ignore the emotions that, at times, threaten to overwhelm. Her book is full of helpful examples and suggestions on how to deal with the various painful steps in the grief journey.

Each chapter includes suggested activities, affirmations, Scripture readings, a prayer, and music you can listen to. At the end of the book there are three appendices offering further affirmations, Scriptures, etc.

This is not just a book to be read. It is a workbook which will help you deal, in practical ways, with the emotions and physical turmoil which caused you to seek after such a resource.

Grief is a part of life, and Yvonne's book offers great suggestions on how to get through those difficult seasons in our lives.

Shirley Corder, Speaker and Author
Strength Renewed: Meditations for Your Journey through Cancer

When I was twelve years old, I lost my father to heart failure. I loved, loved, loved *Moving from Broken to Beautiful® through Grief*. As I read it, I wanted to yell yes! with each thoughtful chapter. Ortega is so raw and honest. Her thought process is clean and easy to follow. It gets to the point without going on and on. The readers will love the practical applications at the end of each chapter.

They are the nuts and bolts of how to deal with one's new life. So often we attend Bible studies, read books and speak to others who are loaded with advice without practical application. This book gives the readers not only relevant stories to draw them in, but also the application which can help them when they have no idea what to do. In grief, we need the gentle hand of one who has gone before us to encourage us to do what may be obvious to others, but through the eyes of grief, it is too hard to see. Yvonne becomes the spectacles, which clarify the way forward. She gently encourages the readers to face their grief. She gives them permission to move forward as needed. We each have "our own way," and her respect and love shine forth in the written word.

Liz Hedger, Rodan and Fields
Bereaved daughter

With her personal, relaxed approach Yvonne takes the pain and grief of loss and makes wholeness seem attainable. As a Joy Restoration© and grief coach, I frequently seek books to help my clients navigate the troubled waters of their grief and loss. *Moving from Broken to Beautiful® through Grief* is moving to the top of my list of "must reads" for my clients.

Wendy Mueller, Certified Christian Life Coach and Joy Restoration© Coach

In *Moving from Broken to Beautiful® through Grief,*

Yvonne has created a window into the world of grief, while at the same time offering hope through practical step-by-step suggestions. Life goes on even when you don't want it to, and this book is a good start at finding a "new normal."

Margaret Sylvia
Bereaved mother

Moving from Broken to Beautiful® through Grief

Book 4

MOVING FROM BROKEN TO BEAUTIFUL® SERIES

Yvonne Ortega

Published by EA Books Publishing a division of Living Parables of Central Florida, Inc. a 501c3
EABooksPublishing.com

ISBN-13: 978-1-945975-30-1 Print
ISBN-10: 194597530X Print

ISBN-13: 978-1-945975-31-8 Ebook

Disclaimer

Neither the author nor the publisher is engaged in rendering medical, health, or any other kind of personal professional services in this book. Before embarking on any therapeutic regimen, it is essential that readers consult with and obtain the approval of their personal health professional before adopting any of the suggestions or drawing inferences from the text. The author and the publisher specifically disclaim all responsibility for any liability, loss, or risk, personal or otherwise, which is incurred, directly or indirectly, because of the use of and/or application of any of the contents of this book. Some names and identifying details have been changed to protect the privacy of individuals.

In loving memory of my mother,
Carlotta Ortega, who taught me how to live.
Also in loving memory of my son,
Brian,
whose journey ended at a tender age.

Contents

Acknowledgements

As I said in *Moving from Broken to Beautiful® through Forgiveness*, this is not a one-woman product. You wouldn't be reading it if it were.

My international online writers' group—Geneva Iijima and Wendy Marshall—critiqued my manuscript from start to finish.

Darlene Barber, Shirley Corder, Cathy Fyock, Sheryl Giesbrecht, Linda Gilden, Carolyn Griffith, Liz Hedger, Rev. Michael Howard, Carolyn Knefely, Heidi McLaughlin, Kathi Macias, Babbie Mason, Wendy Mueller, Sheryl Roush, Karen Schlender, Laura Seibert, Linda Evans Shepherd, Margaret Silvia, Vonda Skelton, and Craig Valentine read the draft of this book, gave me their valuable feedback, and endorsed *Moving from Broken to Beautiful® through Grief.*

Karen Schlender has critiqued my last three books word by word.

Sheryl Roush, an Accredited Speaker and my business speaking coach, told me at least six or seven times not to take on more than I could handle. Each time, I considered another project or position, she would say, "Do you know what's involved in that?" After I answered her, she would say, "And what else?" She made me think by asking me at least three or four more times. By then, I knew I couldn't take on one more responsibility. I wouldn't have finished this book, or my previous one, without Sheryl. I can still hear her saying, "And what else?"

Cathy Fyock, my writing coach, gave the

writers' group writing prompts each session via webinar and told us to link the prompt to our writing topic. I did mine on grief. She also held two writing contests over the Christmas season: one to see who wrote the most words and another to see who finished the rough draft of their manuscript by January 9, 2017. I entered both contests. Cathy dangled prizes over our heads and hooked me. I completed the most words and finished my rough draft.

Craig Valentine, my speaker coach and the person who co-facilitated the World Class Speaking class, encouraged me to share my story and taught me how to share it in his speaker boot camps, individual coaching, and through his products.

Numerous Toastmasters clubs allowed me to present speeches from my book chapters at their meetings.

Nancy Jo Gibson, Michelle Hollingshead, Geneva Iijima, Jean, Louise Tucker Jones, Amy Voltaire, and Denise Wozniak graciously shared their stories with me for this book.

Nanette Snipes, my professional editor from FaithWorks Editorial, edited my book. Thank you, Nan, for not only editing this book, but also my first and second books in the series, *Moving from Broken to Beautiful®*.

The staff at EA Books Publishing guided me in the process from manuscript to published book and e-book.

My friends in the Advanced Writers and Speakers Association (AWSA), my AWSA mastermind group, the Christian Communicators

(CC), my church, and my Women's Ministry Bible Study prayed for me. I needed those prayers, especially when I had a hard drive crash and printer problems. My lifelong friend, Sharron, prayed for me daily and encouraged me on every phone call until just before she passed away in February 2017.

My friends in my aqua classes listened to my manuscript updates and encouraged me.

I don't like cold weather, snow, and ice, but that weather kept me inside when the streets were dangerous and newscasters repeated their warnings to stay off the roads. After one driver died on an icy road, I didn't need a second warning. I stayed home and worked on the manuscript. What else could I do? My activities were cancelled, the gym was closed, and I couldn't get out of my driveway, much less the neighborhood.

My late mother was my best friend, my cheerleader, and my encourager. When I wrote my first book, she took it in a plastic bag everywhere she went to show it off and brag about her daughter, the author. I miss her so much, but her words of encouragement remain in my mind and rest in my heart.

My dad has supported my endeavors in education, speaking, and writing. Although his health has declined, I can still hear him saying, "I'm already proud of you."

And finally, dear readers, thank you for reading this book.

Introduction

Dear reader, you have started the challenging journey of grief. I congratulate you for taking this step. It is not an easy one. You may feel you're all alone on this journey, but you aren't.

You may feel that no one understands you, but many people have suffered devastating losses, including me. Seven years ago, I suffered the loss of two aunts, my mother, and my only child within a span of seven months.

You may think your life is over, and you can't possibly go on without your loved one. I understand. I once felt that way too.

Maybe you've suffered from the side effects of a life-threatening illness, a domestic violence relationship, or sexual assault. Perhaps you're feeling crushed from a divorce, and you can't imagine being single again or dating again. Maybe you've lost a job, a car, or a home. Loss in one form or another has been around for thousands of years since Adam and Eve were banished from the garden of Eden and their son Cain killed his brother Abel. The difference is what you do with that loss.

Although I am a licensed professional counselor, I look at the grief process not only from a clinical perspective, but also from a personal one because of my experience with multiple family losses. No one can rush you through the grief process. You will ride the emotional roller coaster of grief and switch back and forth from one emotion to the other. Your experience will not be linear, in which you go through anger once, get over it, and move on to the next emotion. It isn't that simple, although I wish it were. If it were, life would have been easier for me. So, don't be hard on yourself and expect the grief process to go smoothly and quickly. The grief process isn't like a Nutri Ninja or a Magic Bullet, in which you place the ingredients in a plastic container, one at a time, press a button, and out comes a "smoothie."

Maybe you read the table of contents or leafed through the pages of this book. You may have wondered if you have enough boxes of tissue for your tears. When I started the grief process, I cried so much that my eyes became bloodshot and my head ached. I wondered how I could have any tears left as I wept once again.

The first time I heard the "New Normal," I said, "I don't want a new normal. I want my son back." God didn't raise my son back from the dead as I wished; instead, he had a different plan for me. With time, I sensed God's presence, his passion, and his purpose for my life. I never dreamed I would leave my full-time counseling job to become a full-time speaker, author, and speaking coach.

Only God knows what he has planned for you, but he is in the miracle business. Nothing is too difficult for him. He can change your life in such a way that it will be beyond your wildest dreams. He can help you in *Moving from Broken to Beautiful® through Grief.*

As you move through this book, you may not want to do it alone. If you have a friend, a family member, or a coworker, who has suffered a loss, you may want to invite that person to join you. It doesn't make a difference if the person lives in another state or country, because technology offers many means of communication. You can use Skype or FaceTime. Perhaps you will consider a free account on Zoom, or set up a free, weekly teleconference call. If you don't know how to use those technological methods, look for the nearest teenager to show you.

To help you get the most from this book, I recommend the following steps:

- For the Activities:
    1. Buy a journal or a notebook.
    2. If you wish, you can do the drawing in a Doodle Pad.

- For the Affirmations:
    1. You can write them on sticky notes and place them on your computer, a kitchen cupboard, or your bathroom mirror.

2. Wherever you place the sticky notes, you can repeat the affirmations throughout the day.

- For the Readings:
  1. You can highlight or underline the readings in your Bible.
  2. You may prefer to write the Bible verses on 3 x 5 cards to carry in your pocket or purse to strengthen you during the day.

- For the Prayer:
  1. You can pray the prayer that I wrote or write your own.
  2. You can use the prayer as a screensaver on your computer.

- For the Music:
  1. After you listen to the music, you may want to write your own song.
  2. If you have children, they may want to help you write one. I would love to hear your songs. You can contact me though my website at YvonneOrtega.com.

- For the Moving from Broken to Beautiful® Moment:
  1. Ask God if what I said about myself could apply to you.
  2. Pause, and listen for God's answer.

- For the Appendices:
    1. The Additional Affirmations and Readings for each chapter will strengthen you as you move through your grief.
    2. The final appendix contains Additional Music links to calm your heart and soul and draw you closer to God.

The activities worked for my friends and me. I hope they will for you, too, and they'll encourage, support, and build you up.

May you find comfort, hope, and peace in *Moving from Broken to Beautiful® through Grief*.

Chapter 1

Strike of the Wound Salters

"When you see your friend or relative, the most basic response is to ask how the person is doing and feeling. The important thing is to let the person talk without comparing, evaluating, or judging."[1]

~H. Norman Wright

I I'll check my email while my leftovers warm in the oven. After a long day at work, I thought I would skim my email, pack a lunch for the next day, and eat dinner. Afterward, I planned to read the newspaper, clean up the kitchen, and go to bed early.

The first email I read was from a friend in California who knew my son. She wrote, "I got the news today about Brian. I am at a loss. I want to be here to help you in any way I can. I know he loved you very much, although he may not have shown it. I know he did love you. My prayers are with you."

My hands trembled as I dialed her number. *What could have happened to my son? Was it a car accident? A work injury?* "Hi, this is Yvonne, Brian's mother. I just read your email. What news about Brian?"

She paused a long time, and then said, "Don't you know?"

"Know what? . . . What are you talking about?"

"He passed away two days ago."

I gasped. My knees shook, and my stomach felt queasy. *No, it can't be true. He's strong. He's a black belt in karate and an excellent swimmer. He can't be dead. Parents are supposed to die first, not the child.*

My friend said, "He had day surgery and went home. The next morning, he went into cardiac arrest and died at home. I'm so sorry. I thought you knew. I'll do whatever I can to help you."

The oven timer went off. Dinner didn't sound like a good idea after all. How could I eat or sleep when I felt like someone just sucker-punched me in the stomach? I must have retreated into shock because I don't remember what happened the rest of the evening. The next morning, I sent an email to the counseling agency where I worked to let them know that because of my son's unexpected death, I wouldn't be at the agency or attend the training that morning.

I cried and vomited throughout the day. One by one, the case managers, therapists, and the agency receptionists came to my house to stay by my side and comfort me. Some of them brought food and juice.

One of the therapists said, "Try to eat a little or sip some juice. We don't want you to get dehydrated."

I tried to eat a bite of a muffin, but I vomited. Later, I tried to sip some juice and vomited again. One of the office receptionists followed me to the bathroom and wiped my forehead. I sobbed as I said, "Oh, Debbie, my son will never walk through my front door again."

My phone kept ringing. By evening, my eyes were swollen and burned from crying so hard. I couldn't explain what happened to my son to one more person. I looked at my coworker, Alex, and said, "Please answer the phone for me. I can't take another call."

He stayed with me several hours. As the evening wore on, he said, "Yvonne, I can't leave you alone."

At that moment, the phone rang, and Alex answered. My friend, Sara, told him, "I'll come spend the night with Yvonne. She shouldn't be alone."

Sara arrived soon with a beautiful new journal for me, and Alex went home. I was in shock, but my coworkers and Sara were kind—and I wouldn't spend the night alone.

I appreciated those who came to comfort me, but I would soon encounter well-meaning people who would have been better off not to have said anything. For the sake of confidentiality, I will call those who added anguish rather than comfort "Wound Salters." The first Wound Salter came to my home with a tray of fruit and said, "We all suffer little losses."

She was a wife and mother. How could she not understand the depth of my loss? I wish she had expressed her love for me instead of trying to downplay my grief. I wanted to scream and tell her, "The loss of a nickel or a dime would be little, but not the loss of my only child." I kept silent. I fought the urge to take the tray of fruit and throw it at her.

A week after the Celebration of Life, the church service that honored my son's life, another Wound Salter walked up to me at church and said, "I heard your son committed suicide."

"No, he didn't," I managed to say.

"That's what I heard," she insisted.

I stared at her and said, "You heard wrong."

That dear woman spoke without thinking. Surely, she would want comfort if she lost a loved one. She wouldn't want a misinformed person to walk up to her and say, "I heard your loved one committed suicide."

I wish she had simply hugged me and not made such a hurtful comment.

A third Wound Salter called to see how I was doing. I said, "Every time I look at his pictures, I cry."

"Just put his pictures away."

That Wound Salter was a wife and mother. Did she think that would take my pain away and stop my tears? Pictures or no pictures, how could I forget my only child?

I wish she had shared a memory of my son, or allowed me to do so, instead of suggesting I lock my precious memories away.

As a bereaved human being, you don't need more anguish. You need comfort. Grief leaves a hole in your heart wider than the trunk of a California redwood tree.

Another Wound Salter said, "At least you know where he is."

She meant well, and I'm glad I have the assurance that my son is in heaven. But I felt as if she tried to tidy up my grief process. I wish she had allowed me to cry on her shoulder. This mama needed to cry.

"But I still miss him. I can't see him anymore, and I'll never be a grandmother." I bit my lip to keep from breaking down in front of her. I would rather have cried alone at home than with someone who didn't understand me.

I needed a kind word, but she said, "Well, I'm a grandma, and I hardly ever see my grandchildren."

Perhaps she thought she was sharing an intimate confidence with me, but her words fell on me like sharp rocks. In that early stage of my grief, I didn't have the emotional capacity to stop and counsel her. I looked at her and said, "At least you have them" and walked away.

I heard the comment, "At least you know he's in heaven" too many times. It did not comfort me. I finally told another Wound Salter, "Yes, he's there, but I'm here. He'll never walk through my front door again, and I can't call him or visit him. Mother's Day, his birthday, and the anniversary of his passing will be difficult enough, not to mention Thanksgiving and Christmas."

I'm not the only person in mourning who has ever had to deal with a Wound Salter. One man unexpectedly lost his young son. A Wound Salter told him, "I understand. My dog died recently, and it was like losing a child."

After several comments from the Wound Salters, I remembered how a widow cried as she talked to me. A few days after her husband's death, one Wound Salter told her, "Into every life a little rain must fall."

"A little rain?" My grieving friend had gone on vacation outside of the United States with her husband. A stranger had shot her and her husband for no reason. Her husband survived the ambulance ride to the hospital and emergency surgery, but he unexpectedly died soon after. She had to make plans to fly back to the States alone, with her husband's body in a casket. She was left as a single parent for their two little boys under the age of ten, and with a limp, a reminder of her gunshot wound. "A little rain?" No, it sounded more like an earthquake, a hurricane, and a tornado all rolled into one.

I wondered if that Wound Salter was related to the one who told me, "We all suffer little losses."

My friend, Cathy, told me about her neighbor who lost her husband. The same week he died, a Wound Salter went to the widow's home and said, "I think your husband wore the same size shirt my son does. I wonder if you might have some shirts he could have." The new widow was stunned, didn't know what to say, and gave the woman two shirts. That Wound Salter returned the next day and said, "Those shirts fit great. Do you have any more?"

Maybe that Wound Salter thought she was helping the widow to get rid of her late husband's clothes.

If you've lost a loved one, you understand what I'm saying. As a bereaved human being, you don't need more anguish. You need comfort. Grief leaves a hole in your heart wider than the trunk of a California redwood tree.

I did recover from the strike of the Wound Salters, and you can too. Take the time to work through the exercises for your recovery from the strike of the Wound Salters in your life. As difficult as it may be, tell yourself they spoke without thinking, and they didn't intentionally set out to hurt you. The Wound Salters I knew were good people who felt they had to say something, but they didn't know what to say. They probably would have been surprised and apologetic if you had told them how deeply they hurt you.

Chapter 1 Activities

- Journal about your shock or pain when a loved one died.
- Make a list of the comments from Wound Salters and write what you wished they had said instead.
- Draw a picture or cut pictures out of magazines that express your feelings.

Chapter 1 Affirmations

- It's okay to have feelings about the loss of my loved one.
- I don't need more anguish right now.
- I need comfort.

Chapter 1 Readings and Prayer

- "The tongue has the power of life and death, and those who love it will eat its fruit" (Proverbs 18:21).
- "Those who guard their mouths and their tongues keep themselves from calamity" (Proverbs 21:23).
- "Like one who takes away a garment on a cold day, or like vinegar poured on a wound, is one who sings songs to a heavy heart" (Proverbs 25:20).

Dear God, I'm almost paralyzed with grief.
Protect me from Wound Salters,
who feel they must say something.
Comfort me when their thoughtless words
make my grief worse.
Amen.

Chapter 1 Music

- Contemporary Music: Messianic Song "The Power of Words": https://youtu.be/_FODbaCReFw
- Traditional Music: "Wonderful Words of Life": https://youtu.be/U7x3OX6v5_o

Chapter 1 Moving from Broken to Beautiful® Moment

When I complained to God about the Wound Salters in my life, he showed me the times I didn't know what to say, but felt I had to say something. I, too, had been a Wound Salter. He reminded me that I didn't do it deliberately, but I had inadvertently hurt others. Ouch! I got on my knees, repented, and realized that through my grief, I would learn compassion.

Chapter 1 Journal **Date:_____________**

Example: If someone loses a loved one, I won't be a Wound Salter. I know how awful it feels.

Chapter 2

Compassion from the Comforting Angels

"Gracious words are a honeycomb, sweet to the soul and healing to the bones."

~Proverbs 16:24

I thank God the world has other people in it besides Wound Salters, don't you? I appreciate all the Comforting Angels scattered throughout the world, especially those who helped me through the grief process and the ones who will be there in your time of need to help you.

When I first received the news of my son's passing, a Comforting Angel hugged me, but didn't say a word. Another Comforting Angel squeezed my hand as we both wept. A third one sat silently with me and allowed me to cry and talk when I could. All three Comforting Angels probably didn't know what to say, but their silent presence and tenderness brought me comfort and hope. That's what I needed. They didn't have to say anything.

I remember the Comforting Angels who hugged me and said, "I'm so sorry for your loss." That was enough.

My son's friends said, "I sure will miss Brian."

They went on to tell me the kind things my son had done for them. For example, one woman said, "It seemed like every time I had problems with my computer, Brian showed up and solved them for me."

She made me laugh because I remembered how my son had also helped me use my computer. Every time I ran into trouble, I would say, "Brian, come help me."

He would yell from the next room, "Now what, Mom?"

I would explain my difficulty, and he would fix it so fast that I had no idea what he had done. I would say, "Honey, tell me what you did. I need to write it down for the next time it happens."

He would sigh and explain it step by step. I cherish that memory, and Brian's friend reminded me of it.

One of the two women who co-facilitated the prison ministry at my son's church on the West Coast said, "He loved the Angel Tree Ministry, which was part of the prison ministry. It ensured that every child of an incarcerated parent had Christmas gifts."

That statement blessed me because I volunteered in the same prison ministry on the East Coast. My son had never told me about his volunteer work with that ministry.

Another Comforting Angel from the prison ministry said, "Brian saw the announcement in the church bulletin that the prison ministry needed so many dozens of homemade cookies for the prison four-day retreat. He called me and said, 'I don't bake, but I'll pay someone to bake as many cookies as you need.'"

She laughed, remembering that phone call. I asked her what happened. She said, "He paid for the ingredients, and the rest of us volunteers baked the cookies."

Those Comforting Angels from the prison ministry wrapped their arms of love around me and touched my heart with their precious memories of my son. Memories I knew nothing about until my son's Celebration of Life.

Other Comforting Angels comforted me not only by their words, but also by their actions. One called and said, "I'll be there tomorrow at one o'clock to clean your house for you."

With a broken heart, house cleaning didn't hold a high place on my to-do list. I let her clean house for me.

My phone rang one day, and it was Deborah from North Carolina. She said, "Yvonne, you shouldn't be alone for Memorial Day weekend. I'm coming up to keep you company."

She not only kept me company, she wanted to take me out for lunch the next day. I told her, "Other people have brought enough food for both of us."

"You've been eating that food all week," she said. "Let's go out for something else. My treat."

We went to an Italian restaurant, and then to the mall to find earrings to go with my suit for the Celebration of Life for my son. With gentleness and understanding, she drew me into conversation. Before I knew it, she managed to get me to smile and laugh.

When she packed to return to North Carolina, I hated to see her leave, but she needed to go back to work. She had brought me peace, comfort, and compassion.

Another Comforting Angel called and said, "I want to fix dinner for you tonight. Do you have any food allergies or foods you dislike?"

In the first month after my son's death, I didn't think about what I would prepare for dinner. I felt like a robot going through the motions of existing. I appreciated the meals and snacks Comforting Angels brought me.

I welcomed an offer from yet another Comforting Angel who said, "I'm on my way to the grocery store, what can I pick up for you?"

Until that moment, I hadn't noticed I was out of lots of basic food items.

When another Comforting Angel called, she said, "I'm going to the bookstore and the post office. I'll be happy to pick up thank you notes and stamps for you."

I needed both and welcomed her offer. Afterward, I reimbursed her for both.

All those acts of kindness in word and deed brought me comfort, relief from the pain, and help when I needed it most.

Take out your pen and paper or use the journal pages provided to work through the following exercises. Remember that these exercises are for you. When I journaled about the kind words and thoughtfulness of the Comforting Angels, it comforted me all over again, and I sent them thank you notes. It can do the same for you, and you'll probably want to send thank you notes too.

Chapter 2 Activities

- Journal about your appreciation of the kind words coworkers or friends said about your loved one.
- Tell the Comforting Angels how much you appreciate their kind actions.
- Ask God to bless those who have helped you in your grief.

Chapter 2 Affirmations

- I welcome the kind words of Comforting Angels.
- I accept help from those who offer it.
- I show appreciation for the Comforting Angels.

Chapter 2 Reading and Prayer

- "Blessed are those who mourn, for they will be comforted" (Matthew 5:4).
- "For he has not despised or scorned the suffering of the afflicted one; he has not hidden his face from him but has listened to his cry for help" (Psalm 22:24).
- "My comfort in my suffering is this: Your promise preserves my life" (Psalm 119:50).

Oh, dear God,
I can hardly function.
Thank you for the Comforting Angels,
who help me with their words
and those who do what I cannot.
Amen.

Chapter 2 Music

- Contemporary Music: "Standing in the Gap for You": https://youtu.be/2kaOkmJmxr0
- Traditional Music: "Day by Day": https://youtu.be/lNVCcph6cnI

Chapter 2 Moving from Broken to Beautiful® Moment

As I thanked God for the Comforting Angels, I reflected on how much their kindness means to me and how I couldn't function without them. Through them I've learned to be a Comforting Angel for someone else. Now, I hug or squeeze someone's hand. I make the call, visit, or run an errand. Before I take snacks or a meal, I first ask if the person has food allergies or any foods she/he dislikes.

Chapter 2 Journal **Date:**______________

Chapter 3

Avalanche of Anger

"Tears and words can express feelings of sadness, depression, longing, anger, hurt, fear, and frustration. Remember that, in the midst of these feelings and their expression, a healing and recovery are taking place."[1]

~H. Norman Wright

"God, where were you when my son was gasping for air and died? Why didn't you stop it from happening? How could you take my son so soon?" I asked one question after another without waiting for an answer. I looked toward the sky, fell on the floor in a fetal position, and sobbed. I cried until I thought I couldn't possibly have any tears left to shed, and yet more came.

On another occasion, I sat alone and felt the avalanche of anger again. "Why didn't you take someone elderly instead? Someone who's led a full life." OK, I admit I first asked, "Why didn't you take my ex-husband? He's led a full life." But then I laughed as I thought that maybe he was asking God the same thing about me.

I sat outside with my Bible and journal. "I want answers, God. Please give me answers."

I sensed God say, "I was in heaven when your son died as I was when my Son died. He never married or had a family either. He died at the same age as your son. As for taking an elderly person or your ex-husband instead of your son, look at Psalm 139:16."

I looked at Psalm 139:16. It says, "All the days ordained for me were written in your book before one of them came to be." *Okay, so an elderly person's time and my ex-husband's time weren't up yet.*

Another question arose during my Bible study. Proverbs 13:22 says, "A good person leaves an inheritance for their children's children." *God, I don't like that verse. I'm a good person because of Jesus Christ. However, my only child passed away before he married and had children. How can I leave an inheritance for my children's children? There won't be any.*

I sat outside with my Bible and journal. "I want answers, God. Please give me answers."

God showed me that he allowed me to mentor several women and comfort the brokenhearted through many organizations.

A friend said, "After my divorce, my twin daughters turned their back on God. One of them said, 'Mom, we prayed and prayed for Dad, and he didn't change. How come? We're done with God.'"

She reminded her daughters that God gave them free will, and their dad chose not to change. That answer didn't satisfy the twins. For fifteen years, my friend prayed and fasted off and on for her daughters to return to fellowship with God. They had finally done that less than a year before their deaths in a tragic car accident. She said, "Yvonne, I looked forward to going to church with them. I wanted to see them this summer." I was angry with God, but I was also angry with myself. *If only I had gone sooner, I would have gone to church with them once again. If only . . .*

I said, "You can't change the past, but you can change the present and the future."

After our son's death, I talked with my ex-husband on the phone. Questions swirled through my mind. I couldn't understand why my ex-husband would tell me that I could have my own service in Virginia. I couldn't imagine doing that without a viewing and without saying "good-bye until heaven" to our son at his graveside service.

I hired a professional videographer to produce a beautiful DVD with pictures of our son from infancy to the present. His father said, "You need to send it in overnight mail to Brian's boss." He explained that Brian's girlfriend could add it to the DVD she was putting together. I couldn't understand why he didn't ask me to mail it directly to the girlfriend, but at least I could add my DVD to hers.

I said, "I'll do that, but she cannot change it."

I paid almost $20 to send the DVD in overnight mail. At the Celebration of Life service, the girlfriend's DVD played, but not mine.

The Director of Bereavement Services sat in front of me, turned around, and said, "Yvonne, I thought you had a DVD of Brian from his childhood on."

I explained how I had sent it in overnight mail for my son's girlfriend to add to hers and knew it had arrived. I didn't know anything after that.

"Do you have a copy with you?"

I nodded and pulled out a DVD in a case from my purse. She took it and hurried to the media personnel in the church balcony to tell them to play it at the end of the Celebration of Life. Before my departure for the service, she and I had discussed that DVD over the phone. I sensed I should take an extra copy of the DVD with me to the church. I was glad I did. However, I couldn't understand what happened.

After the service, I asked my son's girlfriend, "Do you have the DVD I mailed to you in care of Brian's boss?" Without a word, she pulled it out of her purse and handed it to me. I wondered why she didn't add it to her video. *Maybe she felt it didn't go with what she put together. I guess I'll never know, but the media personnel did play my DVD. That's what counts.*

At the Celebration of Life service during the

eulogy time, Lacy, one of Brian's friends and one of the co-facilitators of the prison ministry, said, "The other co-facilitator of the prison ministry and I had once interviewed Brian. I asked him why he wanted to be in the prison ministry. He said, 'My mother was my role model. She said that God loves the prisoners, and Jesus died on the cross for them too.'"

After the church service, Lacy said, "Yvonne, I know you must be proud of your son. He did a lot for the prison ministry." Yes, I was proud of him.

After the service, my ex-husband cried uncontrollably. He could hardly speak to thank those who attended. Although I said nothing, I looked at him in disbelief. I had never seen him cry that hard.

At the reception, one of my ex-husband's siblings sat by me, and we talked for a while. I hadn't seen him in years. I gave the copy of the DVD from my son's girlfriend to Brian's father, and he thanked me.

Because I had eaten breakfast early that morning, I was starving by late afternoon at the reception. My ex-husband had arranged for a caterer to deliver an assortment of finger foods. Everything looked inviting and tasted great. My ex-husband asked my friend and me if we wanted to take any of the leftover food with us when we left. We were grateful, and both of us fixed a plate.

The following day, I attended the service at the cemetery and felt the avalanche of anger again. I hated the fact that my son was cremated before his burial. His father had told me over the phone, "That's the only way he can be buried there. There's no more room for caskets." I knew how important it was to him to have the burial at that cemetery, so I said nothing. In the end, it didn't matter to me where he was buried.

I knew his father planned to take the large American flag at the graveside service. So, I said, "Could I take the little flag over the urn?"

He said, "No." I didn't like his answer, but he's the one who paid for the service and the reception the day before. I guess he thought both flags belonged to him.

At that moment, I felt angry. Although I kept silent, my thoughts were anything but sweet.

After the service at the cemetery, I heard my

ex-husband say, "I've hugged everyone but you." I had my back to him and didn't know to whom he was talking. I was not at all prepared when he suddenly leaned his head on my shoulder and sobbed. I would have liked to push his head off my shoulder and scream, "Don't touch me!" After all, his second wife and their child were there. They each had two shoulders. He could have leaned on one of theirs. I didn't say what I felt, but instead stood stoic. The irony was that the Director of Bereavement Services looked at us and said, "A lot of healing took place today."

If she only knew what I was thinking! At that moment, I felt as though a scab from a wound had been yanked from my heart. I wish I had turned around and left.

When I sat alone with God, I said, "Why did my ex-husband lean his head on my shoulder and sob?"

I sensed God say, "It was his small way of apologizing."

In my pain and pride, I said, "His apology was way too small for me."

When I returned home, I was upset with

myself. I had forgiven my ex-husband in the past. I had worked hard for seven and a half years to forgive him. I had journaled, prayed, and participated in a divorce recovery group. I had gone through individual counseling, fasted, and completed Dr. Neil Anderson's *The Steps to Freedom in Christ.*

What happened to all that hard work? Did my pain and pride get in the way? When Brian was alive, he had confirmed my forgiveness of his father. He would call and ask me to pray for his father and stepmother, and I did. I knew from experience that I didn't want to live with that anger. My friend, Arleta, often said, "Anger imprisons you, but forgiveness frees you."

What God showed me is that I had forgiven my ex-husband up to the death of our only child. I felt angry about new things. I had to work my way through the process of forgiveness again, but this time it went faster. I knew too well the physical, emotional, and spiritual consequences of unforgiveness. I didn't want them to ruin my life and my relationships, especially with the Lord. As I said in *Moving from Broken to Beautiful® through*

Forgiveness, "I didn't want to be a prisoner of the past or a victim paralyzed with self-pity."[2]

"Anger imprisons you, but forgiveness frees you."

For about a year, I did well with my anger. But on a flight to Florida to attend a conference, I realized I was also angry with my late son. *Why did he die without saying good-bye to me? Why did he leave me alone?* I talked about that anger with two friends over lunch, and my eyes welled with tears. Later as I sat and journaled, two questions raced through my mind. *Do you think he chose to die that young? Do you think he went to bed that night and said, "I think I'll die without saying good-bye to my mother and leave her alone."?*

I knew the answer to those questions and processed that anger faster than the anger toward my ex-husband. I also remembered something my Sunday school teacher often said, "Forgiveness is for you." As I said earlier, I didn't want any of the consequences of unforgiveness that I suffered in the past. I would get rid of the anger with God's grace and forgive, and I did.

In your grief process, you will experience

anger, at one time or another, the way I did. However, you, too, can forgive. With God's grace, you can even forgive what seems impossible on your own. As you do the following exercises, you can reduce the load of anger you carry.

Chapter 3 Activities

- Journal about your feelings of anger in your season of grief.
- Draw or find pictures in a magazine that express your anger.
- Talk with a trustworthy friend, mentor, or counselor about your feelings.

Chapter 3 Affirmations

- I can tell God how angry I am, and he will still love me.
- My anger is part of the grief process.
- I will not be angry forever.

Chapter 3 Reading and Prayer

- "The Lord is a refuge for the oppressed, a stronghold in times of trouble" (Psalm 9:9).
- "There is a time for everything, and a season for every activity under the heavens" (Ecclesiastes 3:1).

- Listen to my words, Lord, consider my lament. Hear my cry for help, my King and my God, for to you I pray" (Psalm 5:1–2).

Oh, God, I'm so angry
that I can't stand it.
Please help me get through this anger.
I don't want to feel this way.
The cost is overwhelming.
But I can't get through it without you.
Amen.

Chapter 3 Music

- Contemporary Music: "Press On": https://youtu.be/IPUP8jenE9I
- Traditional Music: "The Only Real Peace": https://youtu.be/RkQ8qMDjkz8

Chapter 3 Moving from Broken to Beautiful® Moment

Looking back on that nightmare of anger, I'm thankful God heard my prayer and showered me with the grace to get through it. If I can't stand myself when I'm angry, neither can anyone else. As for that little flag on my son's urn, I could buy one for a dollar. Yes, it hurt not to receive the one at the cemetery. But, I couldn't justify that anger over one dollar. Carrying that load of anger would have given me spiritual osteoporosis.

Chapter 3 Journal **Date:**______________

Chapter 4

Torrent of Tears

"When David and his men saw the ruins and realized what had happened to their families, they wept until they could weep no more."

~I Samuel 30:3-4 (NLT)

Do you wonder if you'll ever stop crying? Do you wake up with tears running down your cheeks? Do you fill your pockets or purse with small packs of tissue? I understand. After my son's unexpected death, I couldn't stop crying.

That first day after Brian's passing, I walked into his bedroom and stared at his pictures and karate trophies. Memories of karate practice together at home left me wiping tears. A few minutes later, I caressed a handful of his medals from swim meets. My tears glistened on the case for those medals. I put the medals back in the case and picked up his Awana Club plaque. He'd received it for memorizing two books of Bible verses in one year when he was eleven years old. The award meant he could go to Awana Camp that summer. The Awana Camp rules at the time required that he raise the money to attend camp. I smiled for a moment as I recalled his conversation with our family chiropractor.

"Doctor, will you help me raise the money to go to Awana Camp? I can't go otherwise." The chiropractor agreed to pay half of the cost, and Brian beamed.

I put the plaque down and glanced at Brian's rocker. I sat down and pictured him as he rocked back and forth on it as a child. I looked at the curtains and pillow covers I had made to match the colors he chose for his bedroom. I never dreamed he would die before college graduation.

I fell on his bed, and my chest heaved with each sob. My son would never sleep in his bedroom again. I felt as if my tears could have filled the Atlantic Ocean.

Grief engulfed me. After what seemed like

hours, I got up from his bed and walked to his bathroom. Fourteen years earlier, he had picked out the bathroom rug and shower curtain. Excitement had filled the air as we shopped that day and went out for lunch. Thoughts of his dying before me never occurred. *Oh, dear God, will I ever stop crying?*

"It's okay to cry. Giving in to the tears is terrifying, like freefalling to earth without a parachute. But it's vital to our wellbeing as we process the deep anguish."

Maybe you've asked yourself if you'll ever stop crying. Maybe you're afraid to cry because you think you must be strong for others.

John 11:35 says, "Jesus wept." His friend, Lazarus, had died. And yet, Jesus would raise him from the dead shortly after weeping about his loss. Jesus was strong, and he cried. You can be strong as well and still cry.

Acts 8:2 says, "Godly men buried Stephen and mourned deeply for him." Surely some of those men—if not all of them—were strong. In Acts 9:36–39, you can read about the death of Tabitha

(Dorcas in the Greek language). Verse 39b says, "All the widows stood around him [Peter], crying and showing him the robes and other clothing that Dorcas had made while she was still with them." Their tears were a normal response to loss.

The death of Martin Luther's thirteen-year-old daughter Magdalene [*sic*] overwhelmed him. He wrote his friend Justus Jonas and pointed out that "while he and his wife should be thanking God that Magdalene was now 'free of the flesh and the Devil,' neither could do so. 'The force of our natural love is so great that we are unable to do this without crying and grieving in our hearts.'"[1]

Maybe someone attempted to shame you for weeping. Years ago, I broke down after receiving bad news. Hard Hannah said, "You're crying? I'm stingy with my tears no matter what happens."

That's not the kind of friend I want in my life. She thought she was strong, but she seemed coldhearted. I wonder why she hid her emotions. What did it cost her physically and emotionally to be "stingy with [her] tears"?

Lynda Cheldelin Fell is an award-winning and international best-selling author and the creator of the five-star series, *Grief Diaries*. She says, "It's okay to cry. Giving in to the tears is terrifying, like freefalling to earth without a parachute. But it's vital to our wellbeing as we process the deep anguish."[2]

Perhaps someone asked you, "When are you going to get on with your life?" A friend of mine had an interaction at church with Insensitive Irma. She told my friend, "Why are you still grieving? Don't you think it's time you get over it and move on? Your grieving is selfish. It's not all about you."

My friend explained to me, "This occurred six months after my father passed away. My husband had been on a six-month deployment, and I had just given birth to my son, my fourth child." It was at that point, she finally asked for help.

Dr. Alan D. Wolfelt is an internationally noted author, teacher, and grief counselor. He is also the Founder and President of the Center for Loss and Life Transition in Fort Collins, Colorado. In his article, "Mustering the Courage to Mourn," Wolfelt says, "To honor your grief is not self-destructive or harmful, it is courageous and life-giving . . . If you do not honor your grief by acknowledging it, it will accumulate and fester."[3]

In my grief process, I recognized that special events like my son's birthday, my mother's birthday, the anniversaries of their deaths, Christmas, Thanksgiving, and Mother's Day are difficult days. I keep plenty of Kleenex on hand and give myself permission to grieve the loss of those I love.

Please give yourself permission to grieve the loss of your loved ones, as I did. When special events or holidays come along, you, too, can keep tissue on hand and grieve. The following exercises will help you get through your grief. As you complete the exercises, allow your tears to flow to help you heal. If you hold them in, one day when you least expect it, they will gush. And they may gush over something unrelated to the loss of your loved ones.

Chapter 4 Activities

- As you journal, express your feelings about crying.
- Buy a few boxes and pocket packs of tissue.
- Listen to soothing music as you mourn. Allow it to comfort you.

Chapter 4 Affirmations

- I give myself permission to cry.
- In order to stay physically and emotionally healthy, I allow myself to grieve.
- I am strong even when I cry.

Chapter 4 Reading and Prayer

- "I am worn out from my groaning. All night long I flood my bed with weeping and drench my couch with tears" (Psalm 6:6).
- "My tears have been my food day and night" (Psalm 42:3a).
- "He will wipe every tear from their eyes. There will be no more death or mourning or crying or pain, for the old order of things has passed away" (Revelation 21:4).

Oh, God, my head hurts from crying,
and my bloodshot eyes are swollen.
I miss __________ so much
that I wish I were dead too.
Please help me get through this pain.
Amen.

Chapter 4 Music

- Contemporary Music: "Save a Place for Me": https://youtu.be/zbsBUf9VKyc
- Traditional Music: "I Need Thee Every Hour": https://youtu.be/tZIMDcgrF-Q

Chapter 4 Moving from Broken to Beautiful® Moment

Because of my own grief, I researched the number of times people in the Bible cried. Men, including Jesus, cried seventy-seven times. The Bible mentions men and women together crying forty-five times. That not only gave me permission to cry, but without any judgment or discomfort on my part, I learned to let others cry in their pain.

Chapter 4 Journal **Date:______________**

Chapter 5

River of Regret

"Have you ever lost someone you love and wanted one more conversation, one more chance to make up for the time when you thought they would be here forever? If so, then you know you can go your whole life collecting days, and none will outweigh the one you wish you had back."[1]

~Mitch Albom

Do you feel like you're drowning in a river of regret? *If only I had told* __________ *how much I loved him or her. If only I had prayed harder, my child might be alive today. If only I had been kinder or more patient with my spouse, maybe he wouldn't have had a heart attack.*

When my son was still alive, we ate dinner at a delicatessen in California the night before I returned home to Virginia. As we talked and laughed about old times, I never dreamed it would be our last dinner together. If I had, we would have talked longer and laughed harder. I would have ordered dessert, so we could have stayed together a little longer.

When my son dropped me off at the airport the next morning, I never imagined it would be the last time I would see him alive. If I had, I would have squeezed him with all my strength. I would have begged him to come home with me, and then made him all his favorite foods. I would have baked him a German chocolate cake and a pineapple upside down cake to celebrate his birthday early. I would have put up the Christmas tree ahead of time and celebrated Christmas every day he was home. I would have put out a new Christmas present each day and stuffed his Christmas stocking with tasty treats.

I cried when I thought of his allergies and drug sensitivity. My mother had a low tolerance for medication, and so do I. My son had inherited that drug sensitivity. I regretted that I hadn't talked to him about wearing a medical ID pendant, sports band, or wristband.[2] Maybe he'd still be alive.

Regret is one of the common emotions in the grief process. I tortured myself with regret over the times I spoke harshly to my son when I shouldn't have or when I spanked him. If only I hadn't done this or that. If only I had been a better parent and shown him how much I loved him, maybe he wouldn't be dead.

Years ago, Jeanette, a teenager in high school, got into an argument with her mother. She wanted to use the car, but her mother had plans to use it that evening and wouldn't let her. As her mother turned to leave, Jeanette screamed, "I hate you, Mom."

Her mother said, "We'll settle this when I return" and left the house. Jeanette realized she had been disrespectful to her mother and stayed up that evening to apologize when her mother returned.

On the way home, her mother lost control of the car, crashed into an oak tree, and died on the spot. Jeanette never had the opportunity to apologize. She said, "If only I hadn't lost my temper. If only I hadn't screamed at Mom." She hung her head, sobbed, and said, "I'll have to live with this the rest of my life."

My online friend, Denise, said, "My husband and I were told our six-month-old daughter, Katie, had AIDS and might live two years. Instead she died three months later." I regret having dreams of what my daughter would be doing in the future—ballet, school concerts, her first birthday, her first bicycle. After her diagnosis, I wished I had enjoyed each second with her, without thinking of the future."

Maybe you're like Jeanette, Denise, or me. You have lots of regrets and can recite your own list of "If only" statements.

When I think about regret in the Bible, I think of Judas Iscariot. Matthew 27:3–5 says, "When Judas, who had betrayed him, saw that Jesus was condemned, he was seized with remorse and returned the thirty pieces of silver to the chief priests and the elders. 'I have sinned,' he said, 'for I have betrayed innocent blood.'

'What is that to us?' they replied. 'That's your responsibility.' So Judas threw the money into the temple and left. Then he went away and hanged himself."

On the other hand, the apostle Peter had disowned the Lord three times before the rooster crowed as the Lord had predicted (Matthew 26:34). However, Peter didn't hang himself. Matthew 26:75 says, "Then Peter remembered the word Jesus had spoken: 'Before the rooster crows, you will disown me three times.' And he went outside and wept bitterly."

In Acts 2:38–41, you see a changed man as Peter spoke to the people. He preached about repentance, baptism, the forgiveness of sins, and the gift of the Holy Spirit. Verse 41 says, "Those who accepted his message were baptized, and about three thousand were added to their number that day."

Peter was not the only one in the Bible to repent and lead a life of power, purpose, and passion. The apostle Paul was formerly Saul, who persecuted the early Christians. Acts 8:3 says, "But Saul began to destroy the church. Going from house to house, he dragged off both men and women and put them in prison."

Paul didn't try to cover up or downplay his past, but he didn't let it determine his future either. Galatians 1:13 says, "For you have heard of my previous way of life in Judaism, how intensely I persecuted the church of God and tried to destroy it."

Paul says in 1 Corinthians 15:9, "For I am the least of the apostles and do not even deserve to be called an apostle, because I persecuted the church of God."

In 1 Timothy 1:15, Paul says, "Here is a trustworthy saying that deserves full acceptance: Christ Jesus came into the world to save sinners—of whom I am the worst."

Though Paul regretted his ill treatment of the Christians, he didn't stay stuck in regret and hang himself as Judas did. Paul repented and lived for the Lord Jesus Christ. He went on to preach the gospel, wrote thirteen books of the New Testament, and made four missionary journeys.

Which path will you choose? That of Judas Iscariot or that of Peter and Paul?

Nancy Jo says, “Even in the most perfect relationships there are things to regret, for we are not perfect. We need to thank the Lord for the good times, laughter, special treasured memories, and release the negatives, the failures, rejoicing that we have such a gracious and merciful God.”

Louise wished she had done things differently. “After my husband died,” she said, “I had all kinds of thoughts of what I wish I had done. It was the same after my son’s death. I finally had to realize that my world was absolutely upside down, and I could not think logically at the time.” Louise also understood that when she began to recall all the wonderful moments they shared through the years, it became healing for her.

I encourage you to sit down with pen and paper, and journal about the wonderful memories you shared with your loved one. As you do that and the following exercises, you will leave that river of regret and experience healing, the same way I did. Rather than take the path of Judas, ask God to forgive you of whatever you've done wrong. Then you, too, can take the path that Peter, Paul, and I took.

Chapter 5 Activities

- Make a list of your regrets and burn it.
- Journal about the good things you did for, and with, your loved one who passed away.
- List the pros of choosing to move forward as Peter and Paul did.

Chapter 5 Affirmations

- I repent of my unkindness to my late loved one.
- I receive God's forgiveness of my sins.
- I move from broken to beautiful as Peter and Paul did.

Chapter 5 Readings and Prayer

- "But God demonstrates his own love for us in this: While we were still sinners, Christ died for us" (Romans 5:8).
- "Very truly I tell you, whoever hears my word and believes him who sent me has eternal life and will not be judged but has crossed over from death to life" (John 5:24).
- "Therefore, there is now no condemnation for those who are in Christ Jesus" (Romans 8:1).

Oh, God, I'm tired of punishing myself.
My endless "If only" statements" make me sick.
Please forgive me for my unkind words and actions.
And help me remember the good times.
Amen.

Chapter 5 Music

- Contemporary Music: "Heal Me O Lord": http://bit.ly/2dGlaC2
- Traditional Music: "In Times Like These": https://youtu.be/j3jK3x3iMOM

Chapter 5 Moving from Broken to Beautiful® Moment

I finally saw the fact that no perfect people exist in the Bible except God, Jesus, and the Holy Spirit. No perfect parents ever existed, or ever will exist, except for God. I can learn from my mistakes as Peter and Paul did and redeem the time for good.

Chapter 5 Journal **Date:____________**

Chapter 6

Sea of Sadness

"Give sorrow words; the grief that does not speak knits up the o'er-fraught heart and bids it break."[1]

~William Shakespeare

I felt so empty and alone after my only child died that I didn't think I would ever smile again. In many ways, I thought my life was over. As I said earlier in the book, I told a visitor, "My son will never walk through my front door again." I felt sad that he died before he had children. I would never be a grandma and have pictures of my grandchildren to carry in a grandma's brag book. I would never be in the crowd of friends who post pictures of their grandbabies on Facebook, and I would never buy gifts for the addition to the family or take a little one shopping. I wouldn't see the smiles on a grandchild's face or hear the squeals of glee as we shopped or as the little one opened Christmas or birthday gifts.

I had learned how to use Skype and FaceTime and had looked forward to seeing little ones on both.

Why couldn't my son have lived? Why couldn't he have made use of his college education? The sea waters became stormy when I thought of his life abruptly ending.

When my mother died before Mother's Day, I felt terrible that Dad hadn't told me sooner that she was dying. He said, "I knew you'd been sick, and I didn't want you to worry."

By the time he called me and had the nurse tell me, "Your mother is waiting to die until she hears from you," it was too late for me to get on a plane and arrive in time to see her alive. I talked to her over the phone. Through tears, I told her how much I loved her. I named one thing after another that I was grateful for. I gave her permission to leave this world, end her suffering, and go to heaven. I said, "Mom, Jesus is waiting for you. So are your parents and your brothers."

Mom was on morphine. She couldn't answer me, but I knew she heard me. Still I was heartbroken that I would never again hear her speak to me or laugh. Mother's Day would come and go, but I could never again call her or send her a card or a gift. Neither would I ever again receive a card, a call, or a gift from her.

I remember Mom as the queen of Christmas. She baked cookies starting in November and baked until Christmas. Mom decorated the house from one end to the other with everything from garlands, poinsettias, and ornaments to floral arrangements, candles, and a Nativity set. She filled Christmas dishes with candy and mixed nuts and kept them filled. She played traditional Christmas carols and more contemporary holiday music. She had Dad string Christmas lights around the house and the garage. What would Christmas be like without the queen of Christmas?

Michelle understood my grief. She said, "I hadn't visited the grave of my younger brother, Matt, since he passed away ten years ago. My heart was broken, and I couldn't understand my grief. I just couldn't bring myself to go to his grave site. I didn't want to go with my mom or my sister, or anyone else and absorb their grief, so I just didn't go."

Amy's grief descended on her at an earlier age. "Cancer took my mother from me when I was eleven years old. She was only forty-two. I had to go live with my dad who was an alcoholic. I remember feeling completely and utterly alone. I'd see girls shopping with their moms, and envy would take over. It seemed unfair that other kids' moms would get to see them graduate, marry, and have children, but mine wouldn't."

"In 1994, I was not prepared at all when I was told my six-month-old daughter, Katie, had AIDS," my online friend, Denise, said. "Katie was also suffering from pneumonia. I learned I had HIV. I was devastated at the stigma attached to people with HIV."

Jean told me, "Patrick's death in December of 2014 came so suddenly. He had not been sick, but he had a stroke that took him away from me. His death left me sad. When a day of being around people is more than I can take, I stay home. I have his ashes at home with me. I can talk with him anytime. When I do, it makes me weep. It only lasts a few moments, but it is very powerful."

I remember eating lunch with Jean on the anniversary of Patrick's passing. Anniversaries are difficult, and Jean thanked me for keeping her company on that day. Memories of the past once again triggered her mourning.

Perhaps, as I have, you've lost a child, and you wonder how you'll survive the sea of sadness. Maybe you've lost a spouse and cannot imagine life without your companion. You go home to an empty house or only one person is in the car—you, and your husband is no longer at your side in bed at night. You may wonder how you'll balance the checkbook and pay the bills without your precious husband's help. You may not know a flathead screwdriver from a hammer, and now you look back on all his maintenance and repairs with a new perspective. You're inconsolable, maybe even overwhelmed, as you think of keeping up the house without your hubby. Maybe you've lost your wife, and you can't imagine cooking all your meals or doing your own laundry. You feel helpless without her.

Although I still have two aunts, two uncles, and cousins scattered throughout the United States, I have only one aunt and uncle left now in my hometown. They call me on FaceTime, send me birthday and Christmas cards, and make me laugh. I feel sad when I think of what will happen when they're gone. My connection with my hometown may well end.

As I write this chapter, my father suffers from dementia. I spent a week with Dad and cried myself to sleep every night. The rock of the family who took care of Mom when she had Alzheimer's is now slipping away. Although he has moments when he remembers and carries on a normal conversation, most of the time he repeats himself. Dad gets frustrated because he wants to be independent and left alone, but he can't be. He also struggles to walk. Although he has a walker and a cane, he forgets to use them. He wears a medical alert for seniors, but he forgot to use it both times he fell backward and hit his head. One of those times, he fell backward on the garage floor! My heart breaks when I see him losing his ability to take care of himself and live alone. As I was writing this book, Dad declined rapidly in the span of three weeks. At this stage of his illness, I won't have him much longer in my life. Tears gush down my cheeks as I think of losing my last parent.

Perhaps you've lost or are losing a family member, a friend, or a coworker. You are helpless to change the course of the loved one's decline. You sob as you face the future without that person. Your feelings, thoughts, and worries are normal. So are your struggles. You're not alone with those feelings and thoughts. Others, including me, have faced the same sea of sadness. We understand.

It's okay to feel the way you do. I once did, but God blessed me with a trusted friend, a counselor, and a pastor. As you discuss your feelings and thoughts with someone you trust, you'll feel better. Working through the exercises, you will experience hope and sense movement out of your grief.

Chapter 6 Activities

- Journal about your sadness.
- Find a trusted friend, a counselor, or a pastor to talk to about your feelings.
- Draw a picture of your grief-stricken face or broken heart. You can cut out pictures if you prefer.

Chapter 6 Affirmations

- My sadness is a normal feeling in grief.
- I can talk about it with the person of my choice.
- I feel safe in talking about my sorrow with those who understand.

Chapter 6 Reading and Prayer

- "He heals the brokenhearted and binds up their wounds" (Psalm 147:3).
- "Surely he hath borne our griefs, and carried our sorrows: yet we did esteem him stricken, smitten of God, and afflicted" (Isaiah 53:4 KJV).
- "The Lord is close to the brokenhearted, and he saves those whose spirits have been crushed" (Psalm 34:18 NCV).

Dear God, I'm overwhelmed with sorrow.
How can I go on without my loved one?
Your Son Jesus is called "A Man of Sorrows."
Right now, I feel like "A woman/man of sorrows."
Please help me. Amen.

Chapter 6 Music

- Contemporary Music: "Broken Hallelujah": https://youtu.be/cH16B5449Iw
- Traditional Music: "Give Them All to Jesus": https://youtu.be/izYol1oBdEg

Chapter 6 Moving from Broken to Beautiful® Moment

I felt like "a woman of sorrows," but I didn't stay that way. The Lord was close to me, and he turned my sorrows into joy through music. The more I listened to praise and worship music and sang it, the more I understood God's reason to command us to sing. It also increased my understanding of the relationship between singing and the heart. Ephesians 5:18–19 says, "Do not get drunk on wine, which leads to debauchery. Instead, be filled with the Spirit, speaking to one another with psalms, hymns, and songs from the Spirit. Sing and make music from your heart to the Lord." Colossians 3:16 says, "Let the message of Christ dwell among you richly as you teach and admonish one another with all wisdom through psalms, hymns, and songs from the Spirit, singing to God with gratitude in your hearts."

Chapter 6 Journal **Date:______________**

Chapter 7

Handling the Holidays

"The holidays don't really come from a store—they come from the heart and soul. Which is why when someone loved dies, the holidays can be so very painful. The heart of the holidays has been torn apart. Without love, what is life? Without the people we love, what are the holidays?"[1]

~Alan D. Wolfelt

As Thanksgiving Day in the United States gets closer, do you wish you could hide until January? Perhaps you would like to fall asleep and not wake up until January 2. Then you wouldn't have to face the holiday season. I understand. I've had those same feelings.

When you read this chapter about the holidays, please know that I refer to the time in the United States from Thanksgiving Day through New Year's

Day. For some, that time frame will extend to January 6, Three Kings Day. It may also include Christmas, Hanukkah, or Kwanzaa and difficult occasions, such as birthdays, anniversaries, Mother's Day, Father's Day, Valentine's Day, and other religious holidays, such as Easter.

Don't be hard on yourself. Give yourself permission to grieve.

The Thanksgiving season my son was two years old, we went to a store known for its beautiful, fresh pumpkins and picked a medium-sized one. He enjoyed it, talked about it, and touched it over and over. Everyone who came to the house heard Brian say, "You wanna see my punkin?" No one refused to see his punkin.

We decorated the dining room table with candle figurines of the pilgrims, an Indian, and two sailing ships. My son would arrange and rearrange them, ask me questions about the first Thanksgiving, and talk to the figurines. I kept them on the dining room table until December 1. They are on the table as I write this chapter.

On Thanksgiving Day, my son and I cut out all

the fresh pumpkin, cooked it for the pie filling and made the crust for an old-fashioned pumpkin pie. By the time we put the pie in the oven, he was covered with flour, spices, and pumpkin. The kitchen floor and the table also showed evidence of a two-year-old at work, but we had fun.

You may select some of your favorite traditions and keep them. You may eliminate others for a year or two, or develop new ones.

On that first Thanksgiving after he died, I didn't leave the house. Friends invited me to their home, but I didn't think I could handle being around other families with their children. If you've lost your spouse, you may not want to be around other couples.

I also missed my mother. I remembered how she would get up early in the morning on Thanksgiving Day and fix a large turkey, mashed or scalloped potatoes, gravy, vegetables, biscuits, and a salad. She had made two large pumpkin pies the day before. Dad loved ice cream with his pie, so that's how Mom served it.

Maybe you have special memories, and you

don't want to leave your house either. That's okay. Don't be hard on yourself. Give yourself permission to grieve. Take time to journal, to listen to music, or to read the book you've had on a shelf for a month. Maybe you'd prefer to look at photo albums, watch videos of your loved one, or catch up on laundry, and other household chores. That's okay too. But please take care of yourself.

You may want to leave your home and serve a meal at a homeless mission or at a domestic violence shelter. That's fine too.

If the Christmas season was a fun time for you with your loved one, you may struggle. It may not be a warm "fuzzy" time of cookies, carols, and cards. The first year or two, you may not want to send Christmas cards or read the happy newsletters that some people enclose in their Christmas cards. Please don't force yourself to do so. Don't pretend to have feelings you don't have. Take the time to grieve.

I remember trying to decorate a small Christmas tree the first Christmas without my son. Wondering what was in one of the boxes, I opened it to find my son's handmade Christmas ornaments and the one that had his baby picture on it. I sat on the floor and cried. Once again, I grieved the loss of my only child.

I remember when my son and I baked Christmas cookies with my Nativity set cookie cutters. He would put more icing and sprinkles on each cookie than there was cookie. We would laugh and talk through our cookie baking adventures and have fun. I couldn't bake cookies that first year after his death. A few years went by before I could.

Dad came to visit me that first Christmas after Mom and Brian passed away. Prior to his arrival, I put out a few of my Christmas decorations. I cried as I pulled out a papier-mâché St. Nick—a gift from Mom, Christmas stockings I bought when we went shopping, and a few Williamsburg Christmas candles. Years ago, Mom had liked my Christmas candles, and I bought her some for Christmas. I had her Christmas placemats and red Christmas napkins on the dining room table. So many memories . . . I remember how Dad and I cried at the dinner table. He stayed a week with me, and we did different things than we had done when Mom and my son were alive. We visited Maymont Mansion in Richmond and Christmas Town, two places we had never seen, and we ate at different restaurants.

Like me, perhaps it will help you to start a new hobby, to go somewhere you've never been, or to listen to a different type of music. You may select some of your favorite traditions and keep them. You may put others aside for a year or two, or develop new ones. It's okay. Take the time to do these exercises so that you, too, can handle the holidays with God's strength and peace.

Chapter 7 Activities

- Journal about your feelings this holiday season without your loved one.
- Spend more time in prayer, Bible study, or meditation to comfort and strengthen you.
- Seek the company of a trusted friend who will listen to you without judging.

Chapter 7 Affirmations

- I can celebrate as little or as much of the holiday season as I choose.
- I can take care of myself and make sure I get plenty of rest during the holidays.
- I can start new traditions.

Chapter 7 Reading and Prayer

- "I am sad and tired. Make me strong again as you have promised" (Psalm 119:28 NCV).
- "I have suffered for a long time. Lord, give me life by your word" (Psalm 119:107 NCV).
- "The Lord gives strength to his people; the Lord blesses his people with peace" (Psalm 29:11).

Oh, God, no calls, no visits, no cards, no gifts.
Help me get through the holidays without ___________.
Show me what to do and what not to do.
Amen.

Chapter 7 Music

- Contemporary Music: "There Will Be a Day": https://youtu.be/CPKyTY71iRM
- Traditional Music: "What Are They Doing in Heaven": https://youtu.be/QtZOY81el8s

Chapter 7 Moving from Broken to Beautiful® Moment

Four years after the loss of my mother and my only child, I felt ready to bake Christmas cookies again, and I baked them with my neighbor's daughter and granddaughter. I shared my memories with the girls as we used the same Nativity set cookie cutters my son and I had used. The girls and I have made baking Christmas cookies an annual event. Afterward, we share the cookies with the neighbors, which is a new tradition for me. Seven years after my family losses, I spent Thanksgiving with friends who have children and did well. I'm glad I waited until I felt ready to do so. The Lord gave me strength and blessed me with peace. And he will do the same for you.

Chapter 7 Journal **Date:**_____________

Chapter 8

Fight against the New Normal

"Human character isn't formed by the absence of hardship, but by our response to the turmoil."[1]

~Cecil Murphey

Have your children reached adulthood? Have they married? Do you have the joy of being a grandparent? If you answered yes to any of those questions, you are blessed.

My child graduated from college and was engaged to be married. However, after day surgery, he went into cardiac arrest. He died of an accidental overdose of the pain killer, Vicodin, which his surgeon prescribed.

Regardless of the cause of his death, I still lost my only child, and I'll never be a grandparent. My life took a different path than what I expected when Brian was first born. If you've lost a loved one, your path has changed too. How do you cope? How do you live the "new normal" when you don't want to? You want your loved one back. How do you fight against and yet survive the new normal?

In this chapter, you will receive the steps you can use to grieve and survive. You will move from the land of fighting the new normal to the land of accepting it.

The first step to accepting the "new normal" is to join a grief support group. A coworker told me about The Compassionate Friends, a support group for parents who have lost a child, regardless of the child's age. Siblings and grandparents are also welcomed. I went, and the people there understood my pain. At my first meeting, I noticed that the attendees placed a framed picture of their loved one on a coffee table. When I went to the next meeting, I placed a photo of my son on the coffee table, too, and sobbed as I sat down. Someone passed me a box of tissues. The Compassionate Friends helped me at a time when I needed it, but they met only once a month. I needed more support than that because of the loss of my mother.

My life took a different path than what I expected when Brian was first born. If you've lost a loved one, your path has changed too.

An energy-saving window salesman came to my home one day to measure for new windows. He saw a picture of my son on my desktop screensaver and asked me about him. I burst into tears and told him my son had died. He told me about GriefShare, a group that meets weekly. I remember my first four GriefShare meetings. I cried on the way to the meeting, from the beginning of the meeting to the end of it, and all the way home. The first night, I cried so hard I couldn't see to fill out the registration form. I had lost two aunts, my mother, and my only child all within seven months. I needed support, encouragement, and hope. The facilitator had also lost his only child, a son. I knew he understood and could help me. I encourage you to join a grief support group. You will meet kind, compassionate people who have experienced, or are experiencing, the same emotional roller coaster of loss that you are.

In *Healing Grief, Finding Peace*, Dr. Louis LaGrand says, "You may be thinking that a support group is not for you, but give it a try, especially if you feel it is a sign of weakness to look for help. Simply being in a supportive, caring environment is conducive to saying what you really feel and might otherwise hold in."[2]

If you attend church or a women's Bible study, you may find encouragement, hope, and support there. My women's Bible study and Sunday school class prayed for me and with me. As Mother's Day approached one year, I couldn't bear the thought of hearing "Happy Mother's Day" over and over. A member of my Bible study group understood, and went with me to the beach that weekend. She helped me get away from the pain of hearing those words.

Now, on Brian's birthday, one of my friends goes with me to his favorite Chinese restaurant. My son loved Chinese food. I ask God each year, "If you eat in heaven, please have someone serve him Chinese food on his birthday."

Friends can ease the pain of loss by being

there for you, listening to you, and taking you to familiar places. My friend, Jean, had lost her dear companion, Patrick, from a stroke. One day, when I knew I would be in Jean's neighborhood, I called her and invited her to lunch. She picked one of the restaurants where she and Patrick often dined on Friday nights or went for Sunday brunch.

The first Christmas season after my son's death, a friend invited me to her church for a Candlelight Memorial Service. She told me to bring a picture of my son to place on the altar before lighting a candle in his memory. I relived the emotional roller coaster of grief, but I also felt the comfort, compassion, and empathy of those who walked to the altar with a picture of their loved one.

My son wouldn't want me stuck in the past. He would want me to move forward. So would my mom.

The second step to living the "new normal" is to journal. At GriefShare, I received a journal notebook and grief devotional for each day of the year. As I wrote each day, I poured out my sorrow, sadness, and hopelessness. In the process, I let go of the fear, anger, and depression. The Compassionate Friends sent a monthly newsletter and also said to journal. I encourage you to journal about your feelings. You can't bury them. They'll keep popping back up, sometimes, in the most unexpected way.

Besides a grief support group and journaling, the third step to living the "new normal" is to move forward in memory of your loved one. My son wouldn't want me stuck in the past. He would want me to move forward. So would my mom. My son had called me BC—Before Christ—because I didn't have a cell phone. One of the first things I did to move forward in his memory was to buy a cell phone and learn to use it. I was so proud of myself when I learned to text and send pictures to my friends that I celebrated my accomplishment with lunch at a restaurant with friends. What can you do to move forward in memory of your loved one?

I followed these steps and moved forward in memory of my loved ones. If you follow these three steps, you can also move from the land of fighting the new normal to the land of accepting it. The following exercises can help you do that. Accepting the new normal will be easier with the help of others. Give yourself a break and allow others to help you.

Chapter 8 Activities

- Journal about your willingness or reluctance to attend a grief support group.
- Ask your friends or look online for a grief group in your area.
- Make a list of the pros and cons of attending a grief support group.

Chapter 8 Affirmations

- I can choose the grief support group I want to attend.
- If I need more than one support group, I will attend more than one.
- I can take a friend with me rather than go alone.

Chapter 8 Reading and Prayer

- "He reached down from on high and took hold of me; he drew me out of deep waters. He rescued me from my powerful enemy, from my foes, who were too strong for me. They confronted me in the day of my disaster, but the Lord was my support. He brought me out into a spacious place; he rescued me because he delighted in me" (Psalm 18:16–19).
- "You saw me before I was born. Every day of my life was recorded in your book. Every moment was laid out before a single day had passed" (Psalm 139:16 NLT).
- "Two are better than one, because they have a good return for their labor: If either of them falls down, one can help the other up. But pity anyone who falls and has no one to help them up" (Ecclesiastes 4:9–10).

Dear God, this journey through grief is a battle.
I struggle to talk about my grief.
Who will understand me?
Who will offer compassion without giving me unsolicited advice?
Who will comfort me without preaching to me?
Show me where to go for help.
Amen.

Chapter 8 Music

- Contemporary Music: "The Hurt & The Healer": http://bit.ly/2fJ69R1
- Traditional Music: "Turn Your Eyes Upon Jesus": https://youtu.be/JbN-7guNHRU

Chapter 8 Moving from Broken to Beautiful® Moment

I learned the power of a grief support group and moved forward because of the compassion, encouragement, and hope both The Compassionate Friends and GriefShare provided. As I progressed in recovery, I didn't cry all the way to the meetings, all during the meetings, and all the way back home. When Joshua and his men fought the Amalekites, the Israelites were winning as long as Moses held up his hands. When Moses got tired, Aaron and Hur got a stone for Moses to sit on and held up his hands (Exodus 17:8–12). Joshua won the battle. God is right. "Two are better than one."

Chapter 8 Journal **Date:_____________**

Chapter 9

Tsunami of Self-Medication

"When a loved one dies, we may rely on many coping mechanisms—healthy and unhealthy—to help us go on living. Some people self-medicate with alcohol and other drugs to deaden their emotional pain. Others, commonly young children, turn to 'magical thinking' in order to deny the reality of the loss and feel more control."[1]

~Susan A. Berger

After Larry lost his wife, he felt lost, empty, and lonely. As an introvert, he didn't want to go to a grief support group although one of his grown children offered to go with him. He felt uncomfortable and unwilling to share his feelings with anyone. He feared others would think he wasn't man enough to face grief. When he could no longer hold in the pain and sorrow of his grief, he turned to alcohol. At first, he drank a glass of wine at dinner. After all, he thought, the Bible says, "A little wine is good for the stomach" (1 Timothy 5:23).

When that no longer numbed the pain of losing his wife, he increased his intake to two glasses of wine. Before he realized what had happened, he would wake up in the morning and drink wine. At lunch, he would have more, and he would continue drinking until he went to bed. Soon, he lost control of his drinking, spent more money than he should have, and withdrew to hide his drinking. His secret came out one day when the police stopped him for erratic driving. He got a ticket for driving while intoxicated and spent the night in jail. That incarceration made Larry realize he needed both substance abuse treatment and grief counseling.

When he could no longer hold in the pain and sorrow of his grief, he turned to alcohol.

Brenda lost her mother to suicide. She cringed every time someone asked her how her mother died. She took on guilt and shame for her mother's death that didn't belong to her. Brenda's mother lived in another state, and she always told Brenda how great she was doing, how she loved her job, and that her boyfriend treated her well. When Brenda visited her mother, she didn't see anything that contradicted what her mother always told her. Her mother's life looked fine. Brenda couldn't believe her mother had deceived her. In addition to the guilt and shame, embarrassment overwhelmed her. She wondered how she could have been so blind.

To avoid the emotional roller coaster of grief and embarrassment, Brenda self-medicated with shopping. She started by buying small items on sale. Soon, she bought clothes whether they were on sale or not. It didn't matter that she didn't need them. She thought shopping helped her cope with her mother's suicide. The company where Brenda worked downsized, and she lost her job. Because her friends and the church staff didn't know about her shopping addiction, they helped her pay her bills and her rent. Within a few weeks, she found another job. Immediately, she went to an expensive store and ordered custom-made draperies for her townhouse.

More than once, Brenda overdrew from her

checking account and had reached the maximum limit on three credit cards. By that time, her friends and the church staff knew enough not to give her any more money. Brenda packed during the night and moved out of the area. Her friends never heard from her again. Self-medication through shopping failed her, and she still hadn't faced her grief.

To avoid the emotional roller coaster of grief and embarrassment, Brenda self-medicated with shopping.

Regina took prescription pain medication for pain from her broken leg. Halfway through the healing process, her sister passed away. Regina couldn't cope with the pain from her broken leg and the loss of her sister. She didn't want to "act like a baby" as she put it, so she lied to her doctor. She said, "The pain is unbearable, and I have to be on my feet more often to take care of the legal matters from my sister's death." She rationalized that she hadn't done anything wrong. After all, the doctor prescribed the medicine, and the doctor increased the dosage. It wasn't as if she were buying pills on the street.

Her leg healed. However, Regina faked a fall in the parking lot at work and "broke" her arm. The doctor again prescribed pain medication. Regina pretended the pain was worse than it was to get the doctor to increase the dosage and frequency of the medication.

After several suspicious accidents and cries about the "unbearable pain," Regina couldn't get a doctor to prescribe more pain meds for her. She bought heroin from a drug dealer on the street. She didn't show up for work, stopped going to church, and withdrew from family and friends. After a third arrest for possession of drugs, Regina went to jail. During visitation, she told her cousin, "This all started because I couldn't face the pain of losing my sister."

Whether it's alcohol, shopping, prescription or illegal drugs, self-medication can become an escape mechanism to avoid the pain of grief. Perhaps, you've turned to food for comfort and have gained so much weight that you've outgrown your wardrobe twice, and your family, friends, and doctor are concerned about your health.

On the other hand, you may have stopped

eating and become anorexic. After Luanne went through a divorce, she stopped eating and looked like a skeleton. Her organs began to shut down. She was dying of starvation until she went to an eating disorders treatment center. With the help of the staff and the participants in the program, she faced her shattered dreams and the coping method that nearly killed her.

Maybe you binge eat and force yourself to vomit—the way Raquel did. She damaged her vocal cords, and her voice sounded hoarse all the time. She suffered from dehydration, fatigue, and hunger. She also had bad breath and dental cavities in addition to anxiety and mood swings. Eating disorders affect both men and women. "In the United States, 20 million women and 10 million men suffer from a clinically significant eating disorder at some time in their life."[2]

Help is available for your grief and for any problems you may have added to it, if you have self-medicated. Kind and compassionate people are waiting to help you. In chapter 8, I talked about GriefShare, a grief recovery group for those who've lost a loved one. At www.griefshare.org, you can find out more about GriefShare and search for a group in your area. I also mentioned The Compassionate Friends, which offers support to families who have lost a child. Look at www.compassionatefriends.org to find the group nearest you and to learn about the Annual Worldwide Candle Lighting and the Annual National Conference. The Center for Loss and Transition at www.centerforloss.org, which I mentioned in chapter 4, offers support to the grieving and to those who care for them. You can ask at group meetings or trainings, if anyone can recommend a grief counselor in your area, and work through the following exercises for your own recovery.

God used GriefShare, The Compassionate Friends, and books from the Center for Loss and Transition to redeem my life. Give the Lord a chance to redeem your life through a grief support group, recovery materials, and these exercises. You'll be glad you did.

Chapter 9 Activities

- Write a letter to the person you lost and tell the person how much you miss him/her.
- Read the letter to a trusted friend, mentor, or counselor.
- Place an empty chair in front of you, pretend it's the person you've lost, and tell the person how you feel.

Chapter 9 Affirmations

- I can express my feelings of grief.
- I can be strong and still talk about my pain and sorrow to a safe friend, mentor, or counselor.
- I can attend a grief recovery group and not lose my dignity and adulthood.

Chapter 9 Reading and Prayer

- "Hear my cry for mercy as I call to you for help, as I lift my hands toward your Most Holy Place" (Psalm 28:2).
- "But you, Lord, are a shield around me, my glory, the One who lifts my head high. I call out to the Lord, and he answers me from his holy mountain" (Psalm 3:3–4).
- "Praise the Lord, my soul, and forget not all his benefits—who forgives all your sins and heals all your diseases, who redeems your

life from the pit and crowns you with love and compassion" (Psalm 103:2–4).

Oh, God, I've tried to run from the pain of my grief.
I didn't want to face the loneliness and loss.
Instead I've made a mess of my life.
Please help me.
Amen.

Chapter 9 Music

- Contemporary Music: "Who Am I": https://youtu.be/mBcqria2wmg
- Traditional Music: "What a Friend We Have in Jesus": https://youtu.be/4XRmGEbH0qs

Chapter 9 Moving from Broken to Beautiful® Moment

The Lord is my best friend. As I read the Bible daily, memorized Bible verses, and meditated on God's Word, the Lord showed me the importance of community, fellowship, and facing my pain. By allowing the Lord to redeem my life from the pit of grief, I could once again eat, sleep well at night, and have fun.

Chapter 9 Journal **Date:______________**

Chapter 10

Fading Faith

"When you are happy, so happy you have no sense of needing Him, so happy that you are tempted to feel His claims upon you as an interruption, if you remember yourself and turn to Him with gratitude and praise, you will be—or so it feels—welcomed with open arms. But go to Him when your need is desperate, when all other help is vain, and what do you find? A door slammed in your face, and a sound of bolting and double bolting on the inside. After that, silence."[1]

~C.S. Lewis

Bob and Mindy were stunned when their seven-year-old daughter, Kristy, received a diagnosis of bone cancer. They were good people and prayed daily for Kristy to recover from cancer. They asked everyone they knew to pray for her. They believed God would answer their prayers and thanked him in advance for her recovery. After all, wasn't God supposed to be a God of love?

Bob and Mindy often quoted Matthew 19:13–15 NCV: "Then the people brought their little children to Jesus so he could put his hands on them and pray for them. His followers told them to stop, but Jesus said, 'Let the little children come to me. Don't stop them, because the kingdom of heaven belongs to people who are like these children.' After Jesus put his hands on the children, he left there."

Didn't this Bible passage imply that Jesus loved the little children and prayed for them? How could he let Kristy suffer through surgery, chemotherapy, and radiation? How could Jesus allow that little girl to lose her hair and suffer with pain day and night?

After all the treatment and clinical trials, the doctor said, "I'm sorry. We've done all we can do. There's nothing left to try. It's time to call hospice."

They asked everyone they knew to pray for Kristy. They believed God would answer their prayers and thanked him in advance for her recovery. After all, wasn't God supposed to be a God of love?

Bob and Mindy felt helpless. They also felt depressed, disillusioned, and distraught. God might as well have been a million miles away. So much for Jesus loving the little children. Their faith faded. With time, they realized that we live in an imperfect world with imperfect bodies. We will all die, some sooner than others. God comforted them through family and friends. Their fading faith turned to a firm faith when they comforted other grieving parents with the comfort they had received from God.

My friend's daughter, Roxanne, loves dogs. When her dog, Wrinkles, got sick, Roxanne prayed each day from the time she woke up until she went to bed. She told family, friends, and coworkers, "I don't have to take Wrinkles to a veterinarian. God will heal my dog." Over a three-week period, Wrinkles got sicker, but Roxanne refused to take her dog to the veterinarian.

The next time my friend saw Roxanne's dog she gasped in horror and said, "Wrinkles is skin and bones. Please take him to the veterinarian." She offered to pay the bill, but Roxanne wouldn't do it. My friend said, "It's okay to see a doctor, Roxanne. In the Bible, Luke was a physician, and he became a disciple of Jesus Christ. He went on a missionary journey with Paul and John Mark. He also wrote the gospel of Luke in the Bible."

When Wrinkles died, Roxanne continued to pray. She said, "I'm not worried. Jesus raised his friend, Lazarus, from the dead, and he can raise my dog from the dead too." (See John 11:43–44).

She wouldn't bury the dog. Three days later, she still hadn't buried Wrinkles. At that point, her husband, Mark, insisted that the dog be buried. She screamed, "Mark, you have no faith. You're not giving God a chance to work a miracle."

In frustration, Mark glared at her and said, "If that's what you call faith, I'll never have it." He shook his head and said, "God did work a miracle. He took Wrinkles out of his pain." Against Roxanne's objections, Mark buried the dog. Roxanne's faith faded. Wrinkles was dead and buried, and Mark would have nothing to do with her church because of its stand against medical care.

After a few years, Mark became a Christian and found a church that didn't preach against medical care. Roxanne eventually joined him in that church, and she now takes their new dog to the veterinarian for shots and checkups.

Last summer, Linda lost her daughter, Laura. My faith faded for a short time. People around the world had prayed for Laura day and night. Many of us had not only prayed but also fasted. We had stayed up late and gotten up early to pray for Laura. Linda is a prayer warrior, and she, too, had prayed and fasted. Why didn't God answer our prayers? Why did he let Laura die? Linda is in full-time ministry. Couldn't God have rewarded her for her faithfulness?

Linda later told me, "It was hard to lose my precious daughter, but through my grief I felt the Lord reminded me that she was no longer disabled. On a particularly bad day, it was as if the Lord allowed Laura to whisper from heaven, 'If you could only see me, Mom, you'd be so happy.' This thought greatly comforted me."

I thought about the day I received a diagnosis of breast cancer and told God, "If this is how you treat your children, no wonder you have so few." That diagnosis shook my faith. You can read more about that in my first book, *Finding Hope for Your Journey through Breast Cancer.*[2] I will say that the morning after my diagnosis, I sang through tears, "The Joy of the Lord Is My Strength." Breast cancer didn't come from God, but he assured me I would live. Every step of the way, he was my strength.

This afternoon, I called another friend, Sharron, in San Diego. We've been friends most of our lives. She said, "Yvonne, I'm dying."

Sharron has pancreatic cancer. When she went for surgery, she entered the hospital with a diagnosis of stage one cancer. The surgeon opened her up and immediately closed her back up. He told the family, "It's stage four and has metastasized to the liver."

Memories of trips back and forth to see each other flooded my mind today. I cried and thought, Dear God, how can you take her so soon? Her husband has dementia and is in assisted living. You're Jehovah Rapha, the Lord who heals. Will you leave their daughters without either parent?

Sharron's diagnosis shook my faith. When I spent a week with her, she said, "Yvonne, I've made peace with my diagnosis, and I'm ready to go home to heaven." Her positive attitude showed me that I, too, needed to make peace with her diagnosis and let her go when the time comes. She had already lost sixty pounds and was on pain medicine. I would rather have her home in heaven with a new body and no pain than on earth in agony. I will miss her when she dies, but I will see her again when I go to heaven.

Seven years ago, God took two aunts, my mother, and my only child within seven months. My two aunts and my mother had led a full life and were much older than my son. I had an easier time with their loss than with my son's. However, daily prayer, Bible study, and memorizing Bible verses ministered peace and hope to me. So did playing praise and worship music and journaling. All those things helped restore my faith. I still remember the morning I woke up real early and sensed my son's presence by the side of my bed. He said, "Mom, don't worry about me. I'm okay. I'm in heaven." That was enough for me. I could embrace the truth that God is good, and his love is both unconditional and eternal.

My father has dementia. God helped me survive and thrive after Mom's diagnosis of Alzheimer's, and he is already helping me through

Dad's dementia. I've met many wonderful people through the Lunch and Learn sessions for caregivers. The speakers provide valuable information and handouts, and the faith and strength of the attendees have restored mine.

Maybe you feel the same way I once did. Life is hard and sometimes seems unfair. But God is faithful, and he will show himself faithful to you. He will strengthen and protect you from the Evil One. Turn to daily prayer, Bible study, and praise and worship music. Also, memorize Bible verses that minister peace and hope to you, journal, and do the following exercises. God will demonstrate his love for you, comfort you, and redeem your losses. Your faith will return and grow stronger each day.

Chapter 10 Activities

- Journal about your fading faith. Be honest with God. He knows how you feel anyway.
- Go for a walk, swim, or exercise in some fashion to release the stress of a fading faith.
- Talk with a trusted friend, a mentor, or a counselor about your struggle to trust God because of your loss or impending loss.

Chapter 10 Affirmations

- I can tell God the truth about my doubts of his love and goodness.
- I will not be struck by lightning for my honesty.
- I will get through this.

Chapter 10 Reading and Prayer

- "A bruised reed he will not break, and a smoldering wick he will not snuff out" (Isaiah 42:3).
- "Yet you are near, Lord, and all your commands are true" (Psalm 119:151).
- "But the Lord is faithful, and he will strengthen you and protect you from the evil one" (2 Thessalonians 3:3).

Oh, God, I don't trust you right now.
I question your love, mercy, and compassion.
My faith is not what it used to be.
I don't know what to think or do.
Please help me.
Amen.

Chapter 10 Music

- Contemporary Music: "Trust His Heart": https://youtu.be/XWk8DRwDYDc
- Traditional Music: "Through It All": https://youtu.be/CvIxwc90BEI

Chapter 10 Moving from Broken to Beautiful® Moment

I learned that God's character doesn't change. As Hebrews 13:8 says, "Jesus Christ is the same yesterday and today and forever." I cannot control God or the world. I don't understand God's thoughts or his ways all the time, but I know he loves me. I can't be like the toddler who says, "Do it my way, or I won't be your friend anymore." On the mountaintop and in the valley, I trust God. Regardless of my circumstances, God is good.

Chapter 10 Journal **Date:______________**

Chapter 11

Acceptance of the New Normal

"Acceptance doesn't mean you would have chosen it or even that you liked it. You have learned to live with it as a part of your life. Recovery doesn't mean you don't mourn occasionally. It means you learn to live with your loss, so you can go on with your life.[1]

~H. Norman Wright

When my mother died, Dad had me help him go through her extensive wardrobe two days after her burial. Her clothes filled all the closets, except one for Dad and one for linen. He said, "Pick what you want to keep. Take what you can in your suitcase. What doesn't fit, I'll take in the car the next time I visit you."

I felt uncomfortable going through Mom's clothing so soon after her death. However, I sensed Dad didn't want to do it alone. He also wanted to take whatever I couldn't use to a needy family that same day. Although he continues to grieve seven years later, he accepted the fact that his wife had passed away.

The presence in my home of some of Mom's clothing and jewelry consoles me. I remember seeing her wear that jewelry and those clothes. When I wear them, I feel close to her.

Three or four years after my son's unexpected death, I accepted the fact that my only child had died, and I would never be a grandma. It still hurts, but not as much. I could move on to what is called the "new normal."

In writing about the new normal, Ethan Gilsdorf said, "Discovering that there's an actual term for how I've learned to live after my sisters' illness and deaths, as well as my father's, is a relief. It's my late-blooming validation of the way I naturally evolved into creating a full life after loss. Grieving never stops, but it abates."[2]

Part of my acceptance of the new normal included praying for six months about whether to leave my full-time counseling job. I had to keep moving forward, so I finally left counseling to become a full-time speaker, author, and speaking coach. My mother and my son would want me to do that. They wouldn't want me stuck in the past. I still remember the Christmas season of 2015. My friend's daughter had a baby boy. I insisted that she take the blue-and-white gingham quilt I had made for Brian's crib to her new grandson. I cried, but I could no longer allow the quilt to sit on a shelf in the linen closet. I still have a few baby things on that shelf, and perhaps one day God will lead me to part with them. When he does, I will, but not before.

I had to keep moving forward. My mother and my son would want me to do that. They wouldn't want me stuck in the past.

My online friend, Denise Wozniak, said, "Because of my faith that my baby, Katie, was in a better place, I wanted to be with her. That was one of the most difficult struggles for me. Every day would take me further away from the time I was with her." Suicidal thoughts took over Denise's life. Eventually, she realized that God was taking good care of Katie. Every day Denise remained on earth, she could talk about Katie's bravery in facing the pain of AIDS and pneumonia. It also meant that she was getting closer to seeing her daughter again.

Denise told me, "That sustains me. 'Yea, though I walk through the valley of the shadow of death, I will fear no evil: for thou art with me; thy rod and thy staff they comfort me'" (Psalm 23:4 KJV).

Denise also said, "I immediately gave away all clothes that Katie had not worn—two bags full— to a friend who gave birth to twin girls, instead of the single child she had expected."

"I kept things that I could smell Katie on," she said. "One day, I came home to find my mother had washed Katie's pillow. I was distraught. My poor mother had no idea that I would often go to that tiny pillow and breathe in the smell of my daughter. I put all other items, even her diaper bag and blankets, into a large chest at the foot of my bed. Sometimes, I open the chest and look at them."

My son, Brian, had a wooden trunk that matched his bedroom set. I packed his Bible memory books, photo albums, and his games in it. I divided the clothes between a family that could use them and a thrift store.

The following summer, my father and I flew to

Alaska to take a ten-day trip by deluxe motor coach, luxury train, and cruise ship. We smiled, enjoyed the adventure, and met new friends, but we both wished Mom and Brian could have been on that cruise with us.

"My younger brother, Matt, passed away three days after his twenty-seventh birthday," my online friend, Michelle, said. Remember that in chapter 6, I mentioned that Michelle hadn't visited her brother's grave since he passed away ten years ago. She said, "He was my confidante through the trials of our parents' marriage and divorce. We tried to make sense of life and listened to each other's aspirations for the future. I loved him for his candidness and his depth."

In 2011, Michelle attended a conference in Las Vegas where they grew up. She rented a car and drove to Palm Mortuary to Matt's grave. She said, "I sat under a tree and shared my thoughts with him. I cried and let the longing for him pour out." Then she looked up and saw a pink Care Bear with a red heart on its stomach hanging from a tree. She said, "I laughed out loud and laughed some more. Matt would have been the one to hang that stuffed animal from the tree." She continued, "I felt him, and I felt at peace."

My friend, Geneva, said she doesn't think her situation is common to most widows. "I have had such incredible support and prayer that I feel very upheld. Daily, I have assurance from the Lord, 'I'm walking through this with you.'" She said she sees constant evidence of that in the offers of friends to help her, in the comfort of the Scriptures, and her sense of God's presence. A couple now lives in her basement apartment. They pay rent, and she pays them to take care of the three-and-a-half-acre property. Her niece lives upstairs with her and provides company for Geneva.

"I am so grateful that my dear husband, Pete, is with the Lord now. No more depression or dementia. Perfect peace." Geneva continued, "I'm being careful to take care of myself." She joined a gym with a pool to get back into shape. She hadn't been able to exercise much when her husband wasn't doing well. Geneva didn't want to be alone for Christmas and planned a trip to Tokyo to be with her oldest son and his family. She admitted that Pete had wanted to go to Japan one more time.

She said, "I'm sorry we couldn't do it together, but I don't feel I should stay home." In the summer, she hopes to take a cruise to Alaska.

What new plans can you make?

"God has me in the palm of his hand," my friend, Jean, said. "He has guided me toward things I never could have seen when Patrick died. I met a man of faith whom I'm getting to know. Finding a new church to attend is important to me. Patrick and I didn't attend church, and that is why I didn't have a traditional funeral for him." Jean ended by saying, "I'm not as sad as I was two years ago. Every day is better and better."

"Other losses were difficult, but the loss of my son and of my husband changed my life forever," Louise said. "I had been with my husband in some way since age eighteen. I married him when I was twenty years old. He was my rock. I didn't know how to live without him." Louise said that after five years, she still misses him with all her heart, but finally learned how to live a happy life, the life her husband would want her to have. Like many grieving widows, Louise thought it would be a dishonor to her husband if she felt any kind of joy.

She finally realized "that if my wonderful husband were here to comfort me, he would tell me to live life, to love others, and to glorify God because that is what he desired with his own life." Louise said, "I also realized that living such a life honored not only God, but also my husband."

I've learned to honor God, my beloved mother, and my son through my speaking and writing. I give God all the glory for my recovery from grief. I keep a gratitude journal and thank him daily for all the blessings he brings my way. Each day I tell God, "I want to do what you want me to do. I want to embrace the opportunities you give me and live life to the fullest." You, too, can keep a gratitude journal and embrace the opportunities God gives you. You, too, can live life to the fullest.

Chapter 11 Activities

- Journal about what you think your loved one would say to help you accept the new normal.
- Draw a picture or cut pictures out of magazines of things your loved one would want you to do.
- Call or meet with a trusted friend to talk about your journaling and drawing.

Chapter 11 Affirmations

- I can accept the new normal and still honor the memory of my loved one.
- I can smile and laugh again without dishonoring my loved one.
- I can love others and know my loved one would want me to do so.

Chapter 11 Reading and Prayer

- "You, Lord, keep my lamp burning; my God turns my darkness into light" (Psalm 18:28).
- "Weeping may last for the night, but a shout of joy comes in the morning" (Psalm 30:5b NASB).
- "If we live, we are living for the Lord, and if we die, we are dying for the Lord. So living or dying, we belong to the Lord" (Romans 14:8 NCV).

Dear God, I don't want to fight the new normal any longer. With your help, I accept it.
I will always love and miss _________________,
But I realize that I can live and love others and still honor my late loved one.
Amen.

Chapter 11 Music

- Contemporary Music: "Lord I Offer My Life to You": https://youtu.be/FTLGBfv4xaM
- Traditional Music: "Because He Lives I Can Face Tomorrow": https://youtu.be/oPW9xYEyijQ

Chapter 11 Moving from Broken to Beautiful® Moment

My life has changed without my mother and my son. I still love and miss them, but I have moved forward. With God's help, I've opened my heart to include others and love them. And once again, I also love life and live it to the fullest.

Chapter 11 Journal **Date:______________**

Chapter 12

Growth through Grief

"Growth occurs through loss. Life takes on a deeper and richer meaning because of losses. The better you handle them, the healthier you will be and the more you will grow."[1]

~H. Norman Wright

How will you grow through grief? Because of your losses, what mission or purpose will motivate you? What legacy will you leave to make the world a better place? "Losing my mom when I was so young," Amy said, "made me realize how important mothers are. That shaped my relationship with my son. We are very close, and he is a fine young man."

My online friend, Denise, discovered her mission when she suffered the loss of her nine-month-old daughter, Katie. As mentioned earlier in this book, Denise has HIV. She suffered from post-traumatic stress disorder (PTSD), which came on two weeks after little Katie's death. Perhaps a combination of her daughter's diagnosis and death, plus her own diagnosis brought on the PTSD. Regardless, she learned to appreciate every day and to live in the present. Denise said, "At first I painted pictures for all my family and friends so they had something of mine. Now, I take photographs and look at life through a beautiful lens."

She also told me, "My sadness at the stigma attached to people with HIV motivated me to speak on behalf of families with HIV." Her new husband encourages her to do so. She is thankful for medication, living in the beautiful country of Canada, and the opportunity to tell the story of the loss of her daughter and her own diagnosis. She realizes how precious every life is and celebrates getting older, which she never thought she would do. Although she lost her own daughter, she isn't jealous of others who have children. She took courses, read articles, studied videos, and researched. She surrounded herself with outstanding friends and business associates, started a society for children who were infected by HIV/AIDS, and helped families connect. Her passion to raise awareness of children with AIDS keeps her going. You can learn more about Denise at www.denisewozniak.com.

Jean said she moved to her own condo, but it is in the same neighborhood where she and Patrick had previously lived. She hasn't let her loss stop her. Jean has gone on with her life. "I've gotten back to my writing, which I had abandoned for a long time," she said. "I was asked to serve on the board of directors for a local charitable organization. I traveled out of town almost every month in 2016 for a new and exciting adventure."

"God redeemed the grief over the loss of my daughter," Nancy Jo said. "To be a listening ear, to cry with, to point to the Lord's faithfulness, to send notes, make calls, or text are what the Lord called me to do." She considers herself "a vessel through which God loves his hurting children and draws those that aren't yet his children to himself." Nancy Jo and her husband help lead a GriefShare support group. She said they receive immeasurable blessings when they "see people come out from underneath the burden of grief and hear them say how much the support group helps them."

"To be a listening ear, to cry with, to point to the Lord's faithfulness, to send notes, make calls, or text are what the Lord called me to do."

"Eventually, I did good things with my life," Louise said. She had lost her dad, one of her sons, her daughter, a granddaughter, and her husband. She continued, "In writing my monthly column for a magazine, I wrote about my feelings and the loss of my husband. The devastation. The grief. The loss of my future and my children's father. I wrote about the love I had for this man through our forty-five years of marriage and how we met as teenagers. It touched readers' hearts. Many widows emailed me about their loss because they had no support system. I started the support group, Wives of Heavenly Husbands." Through her writing and "Wives of Heavenly Husbands", Louise comforts others who have lost their husbands.

Somehow, I, too, had to make sense of my

multiple family losses. They couldn't be in vain. How could I make sense of losing my mother? She had helped thousands of teachers, students, and entire school districts through her expertise in grant writing. She had helped twenty-six women complete a college degree, obtain a teaching credential, and gain employment as teachers. What could I do differently that would improve the lives of others? Life could no longer be only about my thriving after grief. My purpose had to be bigger than that. I became more consistent in my blog posts and in encouraging adults to be and do all God meant them to be and do.

My son used to talk about what he would do after he retired. He would travel wherever he wanted to go. He would buy a house for me, and the list went on. But he didn't live long enough to retire. I used to say that after I retired, I would become a full-time speaker and author. The sudden death of my son made me realize that I wasn't promised tomorrow either. If I wanted to become a full-time speaker and author, I couldn't put that dream off any longer. Six months after my son's death, I left the counseling job I enjoyed to pursue my dream with all my heart and soul. I attended more speaker conferences and speaker boot camps than ever before. I became a certified World Class Speaking Coach. Speaker Coach Sheryl Roush advised me to obtain my LLC—Limited Liability Company, and the registration of my brand, *Moving from Broken to Beautiful®*. She worked with me to update my speaker one sheet with a list of my speaking topics and my business cards. My new webmaster revamped my website.

What could I do differently that would improve the lives of others?

I never dreamed I would hold special speaker seminars to help other speakers, authors, and entrepreneurs improve their speaking skills to enhance their business. My mom helped others to become professionals, and I, too, am doing the same.

In April 2015, I published my second book, *Moving from Broken to Beautiful®: 9 Life Lessons to Help You Move Forward*. I wanted to leave a written legacy to help others. The traumatic divorce, single parenting, breast cancer, and grief I experienced would finally serve a purpose. Other adults needed to know how they could move forward regardless of life's challenges and transitions. I met Cathy Fyock, the Business Book Strategist, when I was almost finished with my second book. She provided accountability, encouragement, and support. Now, I'm her partner on the webinars.

In May 2016, I published my third book, *Moving from Broken to Beautiful® through Forgiveness*. I wanted adults to know they could break free from the prison of the past and gain the peace, freedom, and abundant life of forgiveness. And now you are reading my fourth book, *Moving from Broken to Beautiful® through Grief*.

If I hadn't lost two aunts, my mother, and my only child within seven months, in addition to going through the shattered dreams of divorce and breast cancer, I wouldn't be the person I am today. Because of those losses, I became kinder, more compassionate, and more patient. I became more willing to share my thoughts and feelings. I grew in my faith because I claimed God's precious promises in the Bible. I would say, "God, your Word says . . . I'm counting on you to keep your word." Sometimes I would tell God, "Your Word says . . . I'm telling everyone about that promise, and I'm counting on you to show up and show off. You don't want to look bad, do you?"

Craig Valentine, the 1999 Toastmasters World Champion of Public Speaking, said, "I couldn't *not* hire Yvonne as the Co-Director of Communication. She hit the road running."

That wouldn't have happened if I hadn't grown through grief. Life is no longer only about me, my community, or my state of Virginia. It encompasses my country and the world.

Again, I ask you the three questions I asked at the beginning of this chapter. How will you grow through grief? Because of your losses, what mission or purpose will motivate you? What legacy will you leave to make the world a better place?

Just as I found purpose and direction in my life after my losses, so can you. To get started, you may have to put pen to paper to take inventory of your gifts and dreams in the Activities below. For best results to help you through your grief, please work through all the exercises. They will help you take the next step to healing as you move forward in your new normal.

Chapter 12 Activities

- Brainstorm ideas for a mission or purpose that will motivate you.
- Pray with a trusted friend or mentor about a legacy you can leave.
- Play easy listening music as you pray for guidance.

Chapter 12 Affirmations

- I can comfort others with the comfort I've received.
- I grow in compassion, kindness, and love for others.
- I can leave a legacy for family and friends.

Chapter 12 Reading and Prayer

- "Praise be to the God and Father of our Lord Jesus Christ. God is the Father who is full of mercy and all comfort. He comforts us every time we have trouble, so when others have trouble, we can comfort them with the same comfort God gives us" (2 Corinthians 1:3–4 NCV).

- “Therefore encourage one another and build up one another, just as you also are doing” (1 Thessalonians 5:11 NASB).
- “‘Comfort, comfort my people,’ says your God” (Isaiah 40:1).

Oh, God, show me how I can comfort others.
Help me to encourage others and build them up.
Amen.

Chapter 12 Music

- Contemporary Music: “Leave a Legacy”: https://youtu.be/Aj2XEcUXdHU
- Traditional Music: “Sometimes It Takes a Mountain”: https://youtu.be/b-24kkrKp1Y

Chapter 12 Moving from Broken to Beautiful® Moment

God gave me gifts and talents, and he expects me to use them. I want to be a good steward of what God has given me. His Son Jesus taught me how to live. He reached out to the world, and I will too.

Chapter 12 Journal **Date:______________**

Appendix A: Additional Affirmations

Chapter 1 Strike of the Wound Salters

- I have friends who will say kind things to me.
- I choose those I want to be around.
- I can leave when someone speaks without thinking.

Chapter 2 Compassion from the Comforting Angels

- I tell my friends what I need.
- I talk on the phone with those who comfort me.
- I open the door to welcome trusted friends and mentors into my home.

Chapter 3 Avalanche of Anger

- I journal about my anger.
- I release my anger without hurting others.
- I talk about my anger with someone who will not judge me.

Chapter 4 Torrent of Tears

- I cry because I miss my loved one.
- I honor my grief.
- On anniversaries and holidays, I keep extra tissue on hand.

Chapter 5 River of Regret

- I cannot change the past.
- I did the best I could with what I knew at the time.
- I focus on the precious memories I made with my loved one.

Chapter 6 Sea of Sadness

- I talk to God about my sadness.
- I'm not alone in my sorrow.
- With God's help, I won't be sad forever.

Chapter 7 Handling the Holidays

- I give myself permission to grieve during the holidays.
- I keep only the traditions I can handle.
- I start new traditions.

Chapter 8 Fight against the New Normal

- I research the grief support groups available in my area.
- I visit them to find the one(s) where I feel most comfortable.
- I don't have to accept unsolicited advice.

Chapter 9 Tsunami of Self-Medication

- I choose to face my grief rather than to self-medicate.

- I don't need an escape mechanism to avoid the pain of grief.
- I exercise control over shopping, food, alcohol, and other drugs.

Chapter 10 Fading Faith

- I talk to my pastor about my fading faith without fear of his condemnation.
- I explain to him or another safe person that I don't understand God's ways.
- I will survive with my faith intact, or maybe even stronger.

Chapter 11 Acceptance of the New Normal

- I accept the new normal.
- I can live life to the fullest without forgetting my loved one.
- I look to God for help to live the new normal.

Chapter 12 Growth through Grief

- I listen to those in the throes of grief.
- I show mercy to the grieving.
- I make the world a better place to live.

Appendix B: Additional Readings

Chapter 1 Strike of the Wound Salters

- "Let no corrupting talk come out of your mouths, but only such as is good for building up, as fits the occasion, that it may give grace to those who hear" (Ephesians 4:29 ESV).
- "There is one who speaks rashly like the thrusts of a sword. But the tongue of the wise brings healing" (Proverbs 12:18 NASB).
- "Let your conversation be always full of grace, seasoned with salt, so that you may know how to answer everyone" (Colossians 4:6).

Chapter 2 Compassion from the Comforting Angels

- "Therefore, as God's chosen people, holy and dearly loved, clothe yourselves with compassion, kindness, humility, gentleness and patience" (Colossians 3:12).
- "Therefore if you have any encouragement from being united with Christ, if any comfort from his love, if any common sharing in the Spirit, if any tenderness and compassion, then make my joy complete by being like-minded, having the same love, being one in spirit and of one mind" (Philippians 2:1–2).

- "Heavens and earth, be happy. Mountains, shout with joy, because the Lord comforts his people and will have pity on those who suffer" (Isaiah 49:13 NCV).

Chapter 3 Avalanche of Anger

- "Make sure that nobody pays back wrong for wrong, but always strive to do what is good for each other and for everyone else" (1 Thessalonians 5:15).
- "When the Lord takes pleasure in anyone's way, he causes their enemies to make peace with them" (Proverbs 16:7).
- "My friends, do not try to punish others when they wrong you, but wait for God to punish them with his anger. It is written: 'I will punish those who do wrong; I will repay them,' says the Lord" (Romans 12:19 NCV).

Chapter 4 Torrent of Tears

- "Oh, that my head were a spring of water and my eyes a fountain of tears! I would weep day and night" (Jeremiah 9:1a).
- "Blessed are you who weep now, for you will laugh" (Luke 6:21b).
- "Hear my prayer, Lord, listen to my cry for help; do not be deaf to my weeping" (Psalm 39:12a).

Chapter 5 River of Regret

- "Those who look to him are radiant; their faces are never covered with shame" (Psalm 34:5).
- "Godly sorrow brings repentance that leads to salvation and leaves no regret, but worldly sorrow brings death" (2 Corinthians 7:10).
- "But if we confess our sins, he will forgive our sins, because we can trust God to do what is right. He will cleanse us from all the wrongs we have done" (1 John 1:9 NCV).

Chapter 6 Sea of Sadness

- "The Lord himself goes before you and will be with you; he will never leave you nor forsake you. Do not be afraid; do not be discouraged" (Deuteronomy 31:8).
- "Why, my soul, are you downcast? Why so disturbed within me? Put your hope in God, for I will yet praise him, my Savior and my God" (Psalm 42:11).
- "A father to the fatherless, a defender of widows, is God in his holy dwelling" (Psalm 68:5).

Chapter 7 Handling the Holidays

- "All my longings lie open before you, Lord; my sighing is not hidden from you" (Psalm 38:9).

- "I lift up my eyes to the mountains—where does my help come from? My help comes from the Lord, the Maker of heaven and earth" (Psalm 121:1–2).
- "Yes, my soul, find rest in God; my hope comes from him" (Psalm 62:5).

Chapter 8 Fight against the New Normal

- "For just as each of us has one body with many members, and these members do not all have the same function, so in Christ we, though many, form one body, and each member belongs to all the others" (Romans 12:4–5).
- "Finally, all of you, be like-minded, be sympathetic, love one another, be compassionate and humble" (1 Peter 3:8).
- "I call on the Lord in my distress, and he answers me" (Psalm 120:1).

Chapter 9 Tsunami of Self-Medication

- "I consider that our present sufferings are not worth comparing with the glory that will be revealed in us" (Romans 8:18).
- "I will instruct you and teach you in the way you should go; I will counsel you with my loving eye on you" (Psalm 32:8).

- "My Father's house has many rooms; if that were not so, would I have told you that I am going there to prepare a place for you? And if I go and prepare a place for you, I will come back and take you to be with me that you also may be where I am" (John 14:2–3).

Chapter 10 Fading Faith

- "Truly I tell you, if you have faith as small as a mustard seed, you can say to this mountain, 'Move from here to there,' and it will move. Nothing will be impossible for you" (Matthew 17:20b–c).
- "May the God of hope fill you with all joy and peace as you trust in him, so that you may overflow with hope by the power of the Holy Spirit" (Romans 15:13).
- "These trials will show that your faith is genuine. It is being tested as fire tests and purifies gold—though your faith is far more precious than mere gold. So when your faith remains strong through many trials, it will bring you much praise and glory and honor on the day when Jesus Christ is revealed to the whole world" (1 Peter 1:7 NLT).

Chapter 11 Acceptance of the New Normal

- "You will keep in perfect peace all who trust in you, all whose thoughts are fixed on you!" (Isaiah 26:3 NLT).

- "I am not saying this because I am in need, for I have learned to be content whatever the circumstances" (Philippians 4:11).
- "For I am convinced that neither death nor life, neither angels nor demons, neither the present nor the future, nor any powers, neither height nor depth, nor anything else in all creation, will be able to separate us from the love of God that is in Christ Jesus our Lord" (Romans 8:38–39).

Chapter 12 Growth through Grief

- "I know that there is nothing better for people than to be happy and to do good while they live" (Ecclesiastes 3:12).
- "We must not become tired of doing good. We will receive our harvest of eternal life at the right time if we do not give up" (Galatians 6:9 NCV).
- "And whatever you do, whether in word or deed, do it all in the name of the Lord Jesus, giving thanks to God the Father through him" (Colossians 3:17).

Appendix C: Additional Music

Chapter 1 Strike of the Wound Salters

- Contemporary Music: "Love Is the More Excellent Way": https://youtu.be/Z9R5-ftzhn4
- Traditional Music: "Thy Word": https://youtu.be/2SLHWFpSlq4

Chapter 2 Compassion from the Comforting Angels

- Contemporary Music: "Compassion Hymn": https://youtu.be/DmRjBnuaH-U
- Traditional Music: "God Will Take Care of You": https://youtu.be/ijytLs96yig

Chapter 3 Avalanche of Anger

- Contemporary Music: "Forgiveness": https://youtu.be/h1Lu5udXEZI
- Traditional Music: "Leave It There": https://youtu.be/iXi3gpVRbCc

Chapter 4 Torrent of Tears

- Contemporary Music: "Jesus You Are My Healer": http://bit.ly/2hDuOV2
- Traditional Music: "Whispering Hope": https://youtu.be/7LkqyC9dMF8

Chapter 5 River of Regret

- Contemporary Music: "What Can Separate You": http://bit.ly/2hUfy9k
- Traditional Music: "Always Go to Him": https://youtu.be/yasuzYyEYMU

Chapter 6 Sea of Sadness

- Contemporary Music: "Jesus, I Believe in You": https://youtu.be/8JrZQgmvrbY
- Traditional Music: "Near to the Heart of God": https://youtu.be/2UnFNHWJ0tA

Chapter 7 Handling the Holidays

- Contemporary Music: "Still": https://youtu.be/z3wwWFsSINQ
- Traditional Music: "He Hideth My Soul": https://youtu.be/GbhzH41V49c

Chapter 8 Fight against the New Normal

- Contemporary Music: "Have Faith in God": https://youtu.be/dqA7Nf1x_Ng
- Traditional Music: "Faith Is the Victory": https://youtu.be/jeE8OCoEgiw

Chapter 9 Tsunami of Self-Medication

- Contemporary Music: "Never Ending Shopping List": http://bit.ly/2i6bF1j

- Traditional Music: "Just a Closer Walk with Thee": https://youtu.be/OOKaircCiGI

Chapter 10 Fading Faith

- Contemporary Music: "Draw Me Close to You": https://youtu.be/IdJBYyNsQd0
- Traditional Music: "'Tis So Sweet to Trust in Jesus": https://youtu.be/-DdgkvnsHjM

Chapter 11 Acceptance of the New Normal

- Contemporary Music: "I Give You My Heart": https://youtu.be/mZGzu6oI9b4
- Traditional Music: "Have Thine Own Way, Lord": https://youtu.be/D29AE8YVSFU

Chapter 12 Growth through Grief

- Contemporary Music: "Power of Your Love": https://youtu.be/SSDWaMK5qFg
- Traditional Music: "Everything Happens for a Reason": https://youtu.be/zyQ5ZSMENF0

Notes

Chapter 1 The Wound Salters

[1] H. Norman Wright, *Recovering from the Losses of Life* (Grand Rapids: Fleming H. Revell, a division of Baker Publishing Group, 1991, 1993), 180.

Chapter 3 Avalanche of Anger

[1] H. Norman Wright, *Recovering from the Losses of Life* (Grand Rapids: Fleming H. Revell, a division of Baker Publishing Group, 1991, 1993), 50.
[2] Yvonne Ortega, *Moving from Broken to Beautiful® through Forgiveness* (Salem, OR: Trinity Press International, 2016), 93.

Chapter 4 Torrent of Tears

[1] Steven Ozment, "Reinventing Family Life," *Christian History Institute 39*: Martin Luther: The Later Years and Legacy Online: *https://www.christianhistoryinstitute.org/magazine/article/reinventing-family-life/* (1993), 5–6.
[2] Lynda Cheldelin Fell, *Grief Diaries: Loss of a Child: A Collection of Intimate Stories about the Loss of a Child* (Ferndale, WA: AlyBlue Media, LLC, 2015). Kindle edition.

[3] Alan D. Wolfelt. "Mustering the Courage to Mourn," Center for Loss & Life Transition. *https://centerforloss.com//2016/12/mustering-courage-mourn/* (Dec. 14, 2016).

Chapter 5 River of Regret

[1] Mitch Albom, *For One More Day* (New York: Hyperion, 2006), Introduction.
[2] *www.medicalalert.org*

Chapter 6 Sea of Sadness

[1] William Shakespeare, *The Oxford Shakespeare: The Complete Works, Second Edition*, ed. John Jowett, William Montgomery, Gary Taylor, and Stanley Wells.(New York: Oxford University Press, Inc., 1986, 2005), *The Tragedy of Macbeth*, Act IV Scene III.

Chapter 7 Handling the Holidays

[1] Alan D. Wolfelt. *Healing Your Holiday Grief* (Fort Collins, CO: Companion Press, 2005), Introduction.

Chapter 8 Fight against the New Normal

[1] Cecil Murphey, *Hope and Comfort for Every Season* (Eugene, OR: Harvest House Publishers, 2010), 22.
[2] Louis E. LaGrand, Dr., *Healing Grief, Finding Peace: 101 Ways to Cope with the Death of Your Loved One* (Naperville, Ill: Sourcebooks, Inc., 2011), 170.

Chapter 9 Tsunami of Self-Medication

[1] Susan A. Berger, *The Five Ways We Grieve: Finding Your Personal Path to Healing after the Loss of a Loved One* (Boston: Trumpeter Books, an imprint of Shambhala Publications, Inc. 2009), 42.
[2] *https://www.nationaleatingdisorders.org/get-facts-eating-disorders.*

Chapter 10 Fading Faith

[1] C.S. Lewis, *A Grief Observed* (New York: The Seabury Press, Inc., 1963), 4.
[2] Yvonne Ortega, *Finding Hope for Your Journey through Breast Cancer* (Grand Rapids: Revell, a division of Baker Publishing Group, 2007, 2010), 29.

Chapter 11 Acceptance of the New Normal

[1] H. Norman Wright, *Recovering from the Losses of Life* (Grand Rapids: Fleming H. Revell, a division of Baker Publishing Group, 1991, 1993), 112.
[2] Ethan Gilsdorf, "Life After Loss Is the New Normal," *Psychology Today* Online: *https://www.psychologytoday.com/blog/geek-pride/201008/the-new-normal* (August 18, 2010).

Chapter 12 Growth through Grief

[1] H. Norman Wright, *Recovering from the Losses of Life* (Grand Rapids: Fleming H. Revell, a division of Baker Publishing Group, 1991, 1993), 33.

About the Author

Yvonne Ortega has not only survived but also thrived after a domestic violence marriage, breast cancer, and multiple family losses including the death of her only child. She has also survived several car accidents, one of which totaled her new car. She encourages audiences that they, too, can not only survive, but also thrive, after life's challenges, transitions, and losses.

Yvonne is a licensed professional counselor, a licensed substance abuse treatment practitioner, and a clinically certified domestic violence counselor.

She is the author of the series, Moving from Broken to Beautiful®: *Moving from Broken to Beautiful® through Forgiveness* (Trinity Press International), *Moving from Broken to Beautiful: 9 Life Lessons to Help You Move Forward* (Crystal Pointe Media, Inc.), and *Finding Hope for Your Journey through Breast Cancer* (Revell). She is also a contributing author to *The Embrace of a Father* (Bethany House) and *Transformed* (Wine Press).

Yvonne has presented writers' workshops from coast to coast in the United States, and she has received a literary award at the Maine Fellowship of Christian Writers in 2002. She also received the Persistence Award at the American Christian Writers Conference in Virginia in 2002, for continuing to write during the time of aggressive treatment for cancer.

She speaks at churches, hospitals, and other organizations. As a bilingual professional speaker, she speaks in both English and Spanish. She presents interactive keynotes, workshops, seminars, and retreats. Yvonne is also a certified world class speaking coach and works with individuals, groups, and businesses.

You can reach Yvonne at www.yvonneortega.com. She loves to connect with her readers through her website and her blog on the home page.

Her hobbies are walking at the beach, collecting shells, listening to the waves, reading, and traveling. Exercise and proper nutrition also play an important part in her life. She uses cell phone apps to keep track of her water intake and nutritional balance.

Connect with Yvonne Ortega

Yvonne's website:
www.yvonneortega.com

Blog: home page of website

Facebook: Yvonne Ortega

Twitter: @YvonneOrtega1

LinkedIn: Yvonne Ortega

YouTube Channel: yvonneortega01

Turn your trial into triumph.
You too can move forward.

"Being true to ourselves is sometimes one of the more difficult challenges in life. This easy to read interactive book helps open our hearts and minds to truths we may have overlooked and helps propel us to a place of wholeness."

Dr. Thelma Wells (Mama T), CEO, That A Girl & Friends Speakers Agency and That A Girl Enrichment Tours, Author and Speaker

Crystal Pointe Media, Inc.
www.crystalpointemedia.com
Available in paperback and on Kindle

Made in the USA
Lexington, KY
04 October 2017